GRAMMAR AND BEYOND 4A

Second Edition

with Academic Writing

Randi Reppen

John D. Bunting

Luciana Diniz

CAMBRIDGE UNIVERSITY PRESS

CAMBRIDGE
UNIVERSITY PRESS

University Printing House, Cambridge CB2 8BS, United Kingdom

One Liberty Plaza, 20th Floor, New York, NY 10006, USA

477 Williamstown Road, Port Melbourne, VIC 3207, Australia

314–321, 3rd Floor, Plot 3, Splendor Forum, Jasola District Centre, New Delhi – 110025, India

79 Anson Road, #06–04/06, Singapore 079906

Cambridge University Press is part of the University of Cambridge.

It furthers the University's mission by disseminating knowledge in the pursuit of
education, learning and research at the highest international levels of excellence.

cambridge.org
Information on this title: cambridge.org/9781108784931

© Cambridge University Press 2021

This publication is in copyright. Subject to statutory exception
and to the provisions of relevant collective licensing agreements,
no reproduction of any part may take place without the written
permission of Cambridge University Press.

First published 2013
Second edition 2021

20 19 18 17 16 15 14 13 12 11 10 9 8 7 6 5 4 3 2 1

Printed in Dubai by Oriental Press

A catalogue record for this publication is available from the British Library

ISBN Student's Book 4A with Online Practice 978-1-108-78493-1

Additional resources for this publication at www.cambridge.org/grammarandbeyond

Cambridge University Press has no responsibility for the persistence or accuracy
of URLs for external or third-party internet websites referred to in this publication,
and does not guarantee that any content on such websites is, or will remain,
accurate or appropriate. Information regarding prices, travel timetables, and other
factual information given in this work is correct at the time of first printing but
Cambridge University Press does not guarantee the accuracy of such information
thereafter.

About the Authors

Randi Reppen is Professor of Applied Linguistics and TESL at Northern Arizona University (NAU) in Flagstaff, Arizona. She has over 20 years' experience teaching ESL students and training ESL teachers, including 11 years as the Director of NAU's Program in Intensive English. Randi's research interests focus on the use of corpora for language teaching and materials development. In addition to numerous academic articles and books, she is the author of *Using Corpora in the Language Classroom* and a co-author of *Basic Vocabulary in Use*, 2nd edition, both published by Cambridge University Press.

John D. Bunting is a Senior Lecturer in the Intensive English Program in the Department of Applied Linguistics & ESL at Georgia State University. Prior to this, John taught EFL in Venezuela. He wrote *College Vocabulary 4* (Cengage, 2006) and worked on a revision of *Vocabulary in Use High Intermediate* (Cambridge, 2010). His research interests are corpus linguistics, vocabulary, academic writing, technology in language learning, and teacher education.

Luciana Diniz is the ESOL Department Chair at Portland Community College and an instructor. She has an MA and a PhD in Applied Linguistics from Georgia State University, and she has been teaching EFL/ESL for nearly 15 years. Luciana's research interests focus on the use of corpus linguistics in vocabulary and grammar teaching/learning. She has presented a number of papers at national and international conferences.

Advisory Panel

The ESL advisory panel has helped to guide the development of this series and provided invaluable information about the needs of ESL students and teachers in high schools, colleges, universities, and private language schools throughout North America.

Neta Simpkins Cahill, Skagit Valley College, Mount Vernon, WA

Shelly Hedstrom, Palm Beach State College, Lake Worth, FL

Richard Morasci, Foothill College, Los Altos Hills, CA

Stacey Russo, East Hampton High School, East Hampton, NY

Alice Savage, Lone Star College-North Harris, Houston, TX

Scope and Sequence

Unit	Theme	Grammar	Topics
PART 1	**Social Responsibility**	**Cause and Effect**	
UNIT 1 page 2	Cause and Effect 1: The Environment and You	Sentence Structure; Common Patterns with Nouns That Show Cause	Sentence Structure: Simple and Compound Sentences (p. 4) Complex Sentences (p. 8) Common Patterns with Nouns That Show Cause (p. 11)
UNIT 2 page 18	Cause and Effect 2: Consumer Behavior	Subordinators and Prepositions That Show Cause; Transition Words and Common Patterns with Nouns That Show Effect	Subordinators and Prepositions That Show Cause, Reason, or Purpose (p. 20) Transition Words and Phrases That Show Effect (p. 23) Common Patterns with Nouns That Show Effect (p. 26)
UNIT 3 page 34	Cause and Effect 3: Social Responsibility	Real and Unreal Conditionals; Common Phrases with *If* and *Unless*	Present and Future Real Conditionals (p. 36) Present and Future Unreal Conditionals (p. 40) Common Phrases with *Unless* and *If* (p. 43)
UNIT 4 page 50	Cause and Effect 4: Alternative Energy Sources	*-ing* Participle Phrases and Verbs That Show Cause and Effect	*-ing* Participle Phrases That Show Effect (p. 52) *-ing* Participle Phrases That Show Cause (p. 54) Verbs That Show Cause and Effect (p. 56)

Avoid Common Mistakes	Academic Writing
Avoiding fragments; avoiding *cuz* and *coz* in written academic English; avoiding beginning sentences with *and* in written academic English	About thesis statements Write an introductory paragraph Avoid fragments with *because*
Remembering the correct preposition in expressions with *cause*, *result*, and *effect*; remembering *of* in *because of*	About hooks Write an introductory paragraph
Remembering the base form of the verb following a modal; remembering the correct form of the modal in real and unreal conditionals	About paragraph order Write an introductory and three body paragraphs Avoid using the pronoun *you*
Remembering to use *result in* and *result from* correctly; remembering subject-verb agreement with *contribute to*	About paraphrasing Write a cause and effect essay Use quotations and references

Avoid Common Mistakes	Academic Writing
Avoiding omitting the relative pronoun in subject relative clauses; avoiding *the same than*	About topic sentences Write one body paragraph (block method) Improving your internet searches
Remembering parallel structure	About supporting details Write one body paragraph (point-by-point method) Avoid using the quantifiers *a lot of* and *lots of*
Avoiding using both *more* and *-er* in comparisons; avoiding using *most* before nouns; remembering *the* in *the same as*	About summarizing Write a comparison and contrast essay Make personal stories more academic
Avoiding *another* in *on the other hand*; avoiding *but* in sentences with adverb clauses of concession	About conclusions Write a comparison and contrast essay Academic email messages
Remembering to use the past participle with the past perfect	About sentence variety Write a narrative paragraph to illustrate a topic Avoid the simple present in narratives
Remembering to use *this/that* with singular nouns and *these/those* with plural nouns	About audience and purpose Write a narrative essay Avoid vague references
Remembering to put the adverb after the modal in passive sentences	About classifying Write an introductory and one body paragraph Irregular plurals in academic writing
Remembering to use the correct form in definitions; remembering to use *who* only with animate nouns	About cohesive devices Write a classification and definition essay Use thought-provoking questions

Unit	Theme	Grammar	Topics
PART 5	**Nutrition and Health**	**Problem–Solution**	
UNIT 13 page 186	Problem–Solution 1: Food and Technology	Present Perfect and Present Perfect Progressive; Noun Phrase Structures	Present Perfect and Present Perfect Progressive (p. 188) Common Noun Phrase Structures (p. 192)
UNIT 14 page 202	Problem–Solution 2: Children and Health	Reporting Verbs; Adverb Clauses and Phrases with *As*; Vocabulary for Describing Information in Graphics	Reporting Verbs (p. 204) Adverb Clauses and Phrases with *As* (p. 207) Common Vocabulary for Describing Information in Graphics (p. 210)
UNIT 15 page 218	Problem–Solution 3: Health and Technology	Adverb Clauses and Infinitives of Purpose; Reduced Adverb Clauses; Vocabulary to Describe Problems and Solutions	Adverb Clauses of Purpose and Infinitives of Purpose (p. 220) Reducing Adverb Clauses to Phrases (p. 224) Common Vocabulary to Describe Problems and Solutions (p. 227)
UNIT 16 page 234	Problem–Solution 4: Leading a Healthy Life	*It* Constructions; Transition Words to Indicate Steps of a Solution	*It* Constructions (p. 236) Common Transition Words to Indicate Steps of a Solution (p. 241)
PART 6	**Social Issues and Technology**	**Summary–Response and Persuasion**	
UNIT 17 page 250	Summary–Response: Privacy in the Digital Age	Past Unreal Conditionals; Phrases Used in Summary–Response Writing	Past Unreal Conditionals (p. 252) Common Phrases Used in Summary–Response Writing (p. 256)
UNIT 18 page 264	Persuasion 1: Violence in the Media	Nonidentifying Relative Clauses; Phrases That Limit Overgeneralization	Nonidentifying Relative Clauses (p. 266) Phrases That Limit Overgeneralization (p. 270)
UNIT 19 page 278	Persuasion 2: Living in an Age of Information Overload	Noun Clauses with *Wh-* Words and *If / Whether*; Phrases for Argumentation	Noun Clauses with *Wh-* Words and *If / Whether* (p. 280) Phrases for Argumentation (p. 283)
UNIT 20 page 292	Persuasion 3: Social Media	Expressing Future Actions; Common Words and Phrases in Persuasive Writing	Expressing Future Actions (p. 294) Common Words and Phrases in Persuasive Writing (p. 298)

Avoid Common Mistakes	Academic Writing
Avoiding the plural with noncount nouns; avoiding *this* in *the fact that*	About emphasizing the significance of a problem Write two paragraphs describing a problem and explaining its significance
Remembering to use the base form of *be* after modals in the passive	About narrowing down a topic Write two body paragraphs for a problem-solution essay Citing sources in academic writing
Avoiding the plural with *for example*; avoiding a comma before *so that*	About evaluating proposed solutions Write two paragraphs related to solutions Use a thesaurus to build your vocabulary
Remembering *to* or *for* after *impossible*; avoiding *than* to introduce next steps	About describing the steps of a solution Write a problem-solution essay Keep an error log
Remembering to use the past participle after modals in past unreal conditionals	About summary-response writing Write a two-paragraph summary-response to an article *In fact*
Remembering the relative pronoun in nonidentifying relative clauses; avoiding *that* in nonidentifying relative clauses	About the introductory paragraph to a persuasive essay Write an introductory and two body paragraphs Use adverbs to avoid overgeneralizations
Avoiding *whether* to express a condition; remembering to spell *whether* correctly	About presenting and refuting opposing views Write two body paragraphs of a persuasive essay Using scare quotes
Remembering when to use the noun or verb forms of *claim* and *argue*; avoiding *according for* and *according with*	About writing strong arguments Write a persuasive essay

Introduction to Grammar and Beyond, 2nd edition

Grammar and Beyond is a research-based and content-rich grammar series for beginning to advanced-level students. The series focuses on the most commonly used English grammar structures and practices all four skills in a variety of authentic and communicative contexts.

Grammar and Beyond is Research-Based

The grammar presented in this series is informed by years of research on the grammar of written and spoken English as it is used in college lectures, textbooks, academic essays, high school classrooms, and conversations between instructors and students. This research, and the analysis of over one billion words of authentic written and spoken language data known as the *Cambridge International Corpus*, has enabled the authors to:

- Present grammar rules that accurately represent how English is actually spoken and written

- Identify and teach differences between the grammar of written and spoken English

- Focus more attention on the structures that are commonly used, and less on those that are rarely used, in writing and speaking

- Help students avoid the most common mistakes that English language learners make

- Choose reading topics that will naturally elicit examples of the target grammar structure

- Introduce important vocabulary from the Academic Word List

Special Features of *Grammar and Beyond*

Realistic Grammar Presentations

Grammar is presented in clear and simple charts. The grammar points presented in these charts have been tested against real-world data from the *Cambridge International Corpus* to ensure that they are authentic representations of actual use of English.

Data from the Real World

Many of the grammar presentations and application sections include a feature called Data from the Real World. Concrete and useful points discovered through analysis of corpus data are presented and practiced in exercises that follow.

Avoid Common Mistakes

Each unit features an Avoid Common Mistakes section that develops students' awareness of the most common mistakes made by English language learners and gives them an opportunity to practice detecting and correcting these errors. This section helps students avoid these mistakes in their own work. The mistakes highlighted in this section are drawn from a body of authentic data on learner English known as the *Cambridge Learner Corpus*, a database of over 35 million words from student essays written by non-native speakers of English and information from experienced classroom teachers.

Academic Vocabulary

Every unit in *Grammar and Beyond* includes words from the Academic Word List (AWL), a research-based list of words and word families that appear with high frequency in English-language academic texts. These words are introduced in the opening text of the unit, recycled in the charts and exercises, and used to support the theme throughout the unit. By the time students finish each level, they will have been exposed several times to a carefully selected set of level-appropriate AWL words, as well as content words from a variety of academic disciplines.

Academic Writing Practice

Students develop valuable skills for college composition and mainstream classes with content based on research of a collection of freshmen writing. The research helped identify grammar features used by writers, and tasks that entering college students are often asked to perform (e.g., compare and contrast, argue a particular position). Extensive writing research also helped to identify the linguistic features that are strongly associated with particular writing tasks. In addition to considering the types of text, *Grammar and Beyond* also considers the function of the task. The section on narrative texts reflect the use of narratives in informational writing, rather than the often-presented personal narratives found in most ESL/ EFL textbooks.

Series Levels

The following table provides a general idea of the difficulty of the material at each level of *Grammar and Beyond*. These are not meant to be interpreted as precise correlations.

	Description	TOEFL IBT	CEFR Levels
Level 1	Beginning	20 – 34	A1 – A2
Level 2	Low Intermediate to Intermediate	35 – 54	A2 – B1
Level 3	High Intermediate	55 – 74	B1 – B2
Level 4	Advanced	75 – 95	B2 – C1

Student Components

Student's Book with Online Practice

Each unit, based on a high-interest topic, teaches grammar points appropriate for each level in short, manageable cycles of presentation and practice. Academic Writing focuses on the structure of the academic essay in addition to the grammar rules, conventions, and structures that students need to master in order to be successful college writers. Students can access both the Digital Workbook and Writing Skills Interactive using their smartphones, tablets, or computers with single log-in. See pages xvi–xxi for a Tour of a Unit.

Digital Workbook

The Digital Workbook provides additional practice to help master each grammar point. Automatically-graded exercises give immediate feedback for activities such as correcting errors highlighted in the Avoid Common Mistakes section in the Student's Book. Self-Assessment sections at the end of each unit allow students to test their mastery of what they learned. Look for [image] in the Student's Book to see when to use the Digital Workbook.

Writing Skills Interactive

Writing Skills Interactive is a self-grading course to practice discrete writing skills, reinforce vocabulary, and give students an opportunity with additional writing practice. Each unit has:

- Vocabulary review
- Short text to check understanding of the context
- Animated presentation of target unit writing skill
- Practice activities
- Unit Quiz to assess progress

Teacher Resources

A variety of downloadable resources are available on Cambridge One (cambridgeone.org) to assist instructors, including the following:

Teacher's Manual

- Suggestions for applying the target grammar to all four major skill areas, helping instructors facilitate dynamic and comprehensive grammar classes
- An answer key and audio script for the Student's Book
- Teaching tips, to help instructors plan their lessons
- Communicative activity worksheets to add more in-class speaking practice

Assessment

- Placement Test
- Ready-made, easy-to-score Unit Tests, Midterm, and Final in .pdf and .doc formats
- Answer Key

Presentation Plus

Presentation Plus allows teachers to digitally project the contents of the Student's Books in front of the class for a livelier, interactive classroom. It is a complete solution for teachers because it includes easy-to-access answer keys and audio at point of use.

Acknowledgements

The publisher and authors would like to thank these reviewers and consultants for their insights and participation:

Marty Attiyeh, The College of DuPage, Glen Ellyn, IL

Shannon Bailey, Austin Community College, Austin, TX

Jamila Barton, North Seattle Community College, Seattle, WA

Kim Bayer, Hunter College IELI, New York, NY

Linda Berendsen, Oakton Community College, Skokie, IL

Anita Biber, Tarrant County College Northwest, Fort Worth, TX

Jane Breaux, Community College of Aurora, Aurora, CO

Anna Budzinski, San Antonio College, San Antonio, TX

Britta Burton, Mission College, Santa Clara, CA

Jean Carroll, Fresno City College, Fresno, CA

Chris Cashman, Oak Park High School and Elmwood Park High School, Chicago, IL

Annette M. Charron, Bakersfield College, Bakersfield, CA

Patrick Colabucci, ALI at San Diego State University, San Diego, CA

Lin Cui, Harper College, Palatine, IL

Jennifer Duclos, Boston University CELOP, Boston, MA

Joy Durighello, San Francisco City College, San Francisco, CA

Kathleen Flynn, Glendale Community College, Glendale, CA

Raquel Fundora, Miami Dade College, Miami, FL

Patricia Gillie, New Trier Township High School District, Winnetka, IL

Laurie Gluck, LaGuardia Community College, Long Island City, NY

Kathleen Golata, Galileo Academy of Science & Technology, San Francisco, CA

Ellen Goldman, Mission College, Santa Clara, CA

Ekaterina Goussakova, Seminole Community College, Sanford, FL

Marianne Grayston, Prince George's Community College, Largo, MD

Mary Greiss Shipley, Georgia Gwinnett College, Lawrenceville, GA

Sudeepa Gulati, Long Beach City College, Long Beach, CA

Nicole Hammond Carrasquel, University of Central Florida, Orlando, FL

Vicki Hendricks, Broward College, Fort Lauderdale, FL

Kelly Hernandez, Miami Dade College, Miami, FL

Ann Johnston, Tidewater Community College, Virginia Beach, VA

Julia Karet, Chaffey College, Claremont, CA

Jeanne Lachowski, English Language Institute, University of Utah, Salt Lake City, UT

Noga Laor, Rennert, New York, NY

Min Lu, Central Florida Community College, Ocala, FL

Michael Luchuk, Kaplan International Centers, New York, NY

Craig Machado, Norwalk Community College, Norwalk, CT

Denise Maduli-Williams, City College of San Francisco, San Francisco, CA

Diane Mahin, University of Miami, Coral Gables, FL

Melanie Majeski, Naugatuck Valley Community College, Waterbury, CT

Jeanne Malcolm, University of North Carolina at Charlotte, Charlotte, NC

Lourdes Marx, Palm Beach State College, Boca Raton, FL

Susan G. McFalls, Maryville College, Maryville, TN

Nancy McKay, Cuyahoga Community College, Cleveland, OH

Dominika McPartland, Long Island Business Institute, Flushing, NY

Amy Metcalf, UNR/Intensive English Language
Center, University of Nevada, Reno, NV
Robert Miller, EF International Language School
San Francisco – Mills, San Francisco, CA
Marcie Pachino, Jordan High School, Durham, NC
Myshie Pagel, El Paso Community College, El Paso, TX
Bernadette Pedagno, University of San Francisco,
San Francisco, CA
Tam Q Pham, Dallas Theological Seminary,
Fort Smith, AR
Mary Beth Pickett, Global LT, Rochester, MI
Maria Reamore, Baltimore City Public Schools,
Baltimore, MD
Alison M. Rice, Hunter College IELI, New York, NY
Sydney Rice, Imperial Valley College, Imperial, CA
Kathleen Romstedt, Ohio State University,
Columbus, OH
Alexandra Rowe, University of South Carolina,
Columbia, SC
Irma Sanders, Baldwin Park Adult and Community
Education, Baldwin Park, CA
Caren Shoup, Lone Star College – CyFair, Cypress, TX

Karen Sid, Mission College, Foothill College, De
Anza College, Santa Clara, CA
Michelle Thomas, Miami Dade College, Miami, FL
Sharon Van Houte, Lorain County Community
College, Elyria, OH
Margi Wald, UC Berkeley, Berkeley, CA
Walli Weitz, Riverside County Office of Ed.,
Indio, CA
Bart Weyand, University of Southern Maine,
Portland, ME
Donna Weyrich, Columbus State Community
College, Columbus, OH
Marilyn Whitehorse, Santa Barbara City College,
Ojai, CA
Jessica Wilson, Rutgers University – Newark,
Newark, NJ
Sue Wilson, San Jose City College, San Jose, CA
Margaret Wilster, Mid-Florida Tech, Orlando, FL
Anne York-Herjeczki, Santa Monica College, Santa
Monica, CA
Hoda Zaki, Camden County College, Camden, NJ

We would also like to thank these teachers and programs for allowing us to visit:

Richard Appelbaum, Broward College, Fort
Lauderdale, FL
Carmela Arnoldt, Glendale Community College,
Glendale, AZ
JaNae Barrow, Desert Vista High School, Phoenix, AZ
Ted Christensen, Mesa Community College, Mesa, AZ
Richard Ciriello, Lower East Side Preparatory High
School, New York, NY
Virginia Edwards, Chandler-Gilbert Community
College, Chandler, AZ
Nusia Frankel, Miami Dade College, Miami, FL
Raquel Fundora, Miami Dade College, Miami, FL
Vicki Hendricks, Broward College, Fort Lauderdale, FL
Kelly Hernandez, Miami Dade College, Miami, FL
Stephen Johnson, Miami Dade College, Miami, FL
Barbara Jordan, Mesa Community College, Mesa, AZ
Nancy Kersten, GateWay Community College,
Phoenix, AZ
Lewis Levine, Hostos Community College, Bronx, NY
John Liffiton, Scottsdale Community College,
Scottsdale, AZ
Cheryl Lira-Layne, Gilbert Public School District,
Gilbert, AZ

Mary Livingston, Arizona State University, Tempe, AZ
Elizabeth Macdonald, Thunderbird School of
Global Management, Glendale, AZ
Terri Martinez, Mesa Community College, Mesa, AZ
Lourdes Marx, Palm Beach State College,
Boca Raton, FL
Paul Kei Matsuda, Arizona State University, Tempe, AZ
David Miller, Glendale Community College,
Glendale, AZ
Martha Polin, Lower East Side Preparatory High
School, New York, NY
Patricia Pullenza, Mesa Community College, Mesa, AZ
Victoria Rasinskaya, Lower East Side Preparatory
High School, New York, NY
Vanda Salls, Tempe Union High School District,
Tempe, AZ
Kim Sanabria, Hostos Community College,
Bronx, NY
Cynthia Schuemann, Miami Dade College, Miami, FL
Michelle Thomas, Miami Dade College, Miami, FL
Dongmei Zeng, Borough of Manhattan Community
College, New York, NY

Tour of a Unit

UNIT 5

Comparison and Contrast 1: Identifying Relative Clauses; Comparatives with *As . . . As*; Common Patterns That Show Contrast

Family Size and Personality

1 Grammar in the Real World

You will read an essay that discusses how a child's birth order in the family may affect his or her personality as an adult. The essay is an example of a type of comparison and contrast writing in which the ideas are organized using the block method.

A Before You Read How many siblings do you have? Do you think that some of their personality traits come from the order of their birth? Read the essay. How strong are the effects of birth order, according to the essay?

B Comprehension Check Answer the questions.

1 How are former presidents Jimmy Carter, George W. Bush, and Barack Obama connected to the main idea of the text?

2 According to the writer, why are firstborn children usually more ambitious than their siblings?

3 Which of the different birth order types – firstborn, middle born, youngest, and only child – do you think has the fewest advantages in life? Explain.

C Notice Follow the instructions below to help you notice and understand comparison and contrast sentences from the essay that use *as . . . as*.

1 Read the *as . . . as* sentence in the third paragraph. Are middle children likely to be equally, more, or less determined than firstborn children? Explain.

2 Read the *as . . . as* sentence in the fourth paragraph. Are youngest children likely to be equally, more, or less creative than middle children? Explain.

3 Read the *as . . . as* sentence in the fifth paragraph. Are only children likely to be equally, more, or less intelligent than children with siblings? Explain.

D Academic Writing Underline the sentence that gives the main idea of each body paragraph. This sentence is called the *topic sentence*.

64

Birth Order
and Adult Sibling Relationships

What do U.S. Presidents Jimmy Carter, George W. Bush, and Barack Obama all have in common? In addition to being elected president of the United States, these men all share the same birth order. Each one is the oldest child in his family. In fact, many very successful people in government and business have been "firstborn" children. While there is always some variation, some experts agree that birth order can have an influence on a person's personality in childhood and in adulthood.

Firstborn children often share several traits. First, in contrast to their siblings, they are more likely to be responsible, ambitious, and authoritarian. This is probably because they are born into an environment of high expectations, and they usually receive a great deal of attention. They are used to being leaders, taking responsibility for others, and sometimes taking on an almost parental role.

Middle children, on the other hand, exhibit different characteristics from firstborns. They are often not as determined as firstborns. They tend to be more passive and solitary. Having to share family attention with older and younger siblings, middle children have a tendency to be more realistic, creative, and insightful.

Youngest children are often more protected than their older siblings. As a result, they are more likely to be dependent and controlling. They are often as creative as middle children, but usually more easygoing and social.

A child with no siblings, or an "only child," also exhibits some unique characteristics. While some parents worry that an only child will have difficulties socializing and making friends, studies show that an only child is just as intelligent, accomplished, and sociable as a child with siblings. In fact, some research indicates that being an only child has some benefits. These children tend to have better vocabulary, perform better at school, and maintain closer relationships with their parents than children with siblings.

Even though it is assumed that birth order dictates some personality traits, individuals can free themselves from the roles they played when they were young, but it can be difficult. According to Vikki Stark, family therapist and author of *My Sister, My Self*, change requires letting go of familiar ways of being and patiently asserting new behaviors that express one's true self (Kochan, para. 14).

Family Size and Personality **65**

2 Identifying Relative Clauses

Grammar Presentation

A relative clause modifies a noun and follows the noun it modifies. Identifying relative clauses provide necessary information about the noun. They are used in all kinds of academic writing, but they are especially useful in comparison and contrast writing to describe characteristics of elements that are being compared.

Children who/that have no siblings are often very close to their parents. People gradually behave in ways which/that are more consistent with their preferred self-image.

2.1 Identifying Relative Clauses

A An identifying relative clause modifies a noun. It begins with a relative pronoun: *that, which, who, whom,* or *whose.* (It is often called a *restrictive relative clause.*)

An identifying relative clause answers the question, "Which one?" It gives necessary information about the noun or noun phrase in the main clause. Without that information, the sentence would be incomplete.

IDENTIFYING RELATIVE CLAUSE
People who do not have children may not be aware of differences in birth order.
IDENTIFYING RELATIVE CLAUSE
Creativity is a trait that all middle children share.

B *Who, that,* and *whom* refer to people. Use *whom* for object relative clauses. In informal speaking and writing, the use of *who* for *whom* is common.

PEOPLE
Researchers who/that study families have different views.
My siblings are the people in my life whom I will always trust.

C *Whose* shows possession. It is followed by an animate or inanimate noun in academic writing.

POSSESSION
Researchers whose work focuses on families disagree about the importance of birth order.
She cited a study whose results supported previous research.

Which and *that* refer to things. In academic writing, *that* is often preferred to *which* in identifying relative clauses.

THINGS
The study examines characteristics that/which are common in firstborn children.

DATA FROM THE REAL WORLD

In academic writing, the relative pronoun **who** is more commonly used than **that** to refer to people.

In speaking, the relative pronoun **that** is more commonly used than **who** to refer to people.

Grammar Application

Exercise 2.1 Identifying Relative Clauses

A Read the paragraph about birth order. Complete each sentence with *that, who, whom,* or *whose.* Sometimes more than one answer is possible.

Birth order researchers have discovered some interesting information <u>*that*</u> (1) can help us understand our colleagues better. Do you have a difficult boss __________ (2) authoritarian personality makes your life difficult? If so, your boss might be a firstborn child. Children __________ (3) are born first are often more authoritarian than their younger siblings. Do you have a co-worker __________ (4) is passive, but particularly creative and insightful? This person may be a middle child. People __________ (5) have both older and younger siblings are often passive because their older siblings were responsible for their well-being when they were young. The creativity __________ (6) they exhibit might be the effect of their having spent a lot of time on their own due to having to share parental attention with their older and younger siblings. People __________ (7) you work with __________ (8) are controlling may be youngest children. These people are also likely to be more social than co-workers __________ (9) are middle children. Of course, these are only generalizations. There are countless factors __________ (10) help form people's personalities, but birth order research may shed some helpful light on people's behavior in the workplace.

DATA FROM THE REAL WORLD

takes students beyond traditional information and teaches them how the unit's grammar is used in authentic situations, including differences between spoken and written use.

QR CODES

give easy access to audio at point of use.

DATA FROM THE REAL WORLD

In academic writing, 75 percent of relative clauses with *whose* modify inanimate nouns.

The report included the results of a study funded by an organization *whose* mission is to help children reach their potential.

Exercise 3.2 Comparatives with *As . . . As*

A Listen to the story of two famous sisters – Venus and Serena Williams. Complete the chart.

	Venus Williams	Serena Williams
1 Birth date	June 17, 1980	
2 Height	6'1"	
3 Year turned professional		
4 Wimbledon singles victories (individual years)		
5 U.S. Open singles victories (individual years)		

B On a separate sheet of paper, use the information from A and the cues below to write sentences with the following *as . . . as* phrases: *almost as . . . as; just as . . . as; not nearly as . . . as* and *not quite as . . . as.* Sometimes more than one answer is possible.

1 Serena / is / tall / Venus.

Serena is not quite as tall as Venus.

2 Serena / has / played / long / Venus.

3 Serena / is / old / Venus.

4 Serena / has / experience / Venus.

5 Serena / is / important to U.S. sports / Venus.

6 Serena / has / won / Wimbledon singles / Venus.

7 Venus / is / famous / Serena.

8 Serena / has had / Wimbledon singles victories / Venus has had.

9 Venus / has had / success in business / Serena. They are both successful businesswomen.

Serena and Venus Williams

C Pair Work Tell a partner about two people you know well. Compare them using *as . . . as* structures. Next, write five sentences about them using *as . . . as.* Use adjectives, adverbs, and noun phrases as well as phrases such as *almost, not nearly,* and *not quite* in your sentences where possible.

Younsil does not have as many children as Victoria.
Younsil is not quite as shy as Victoria.

HOW TO USE A QR CODE

1 Open the camera on your smartphone.

2 Point it at the QR code.

3 The camera will automatically scan the code. If not, press the button to take a picture.

* Not all cameras automatically scan QR codes. You may need to download a QR code reader. Search "QR free" and download an app.

Vocabulary Application

Exercise 4.1 Vocabulary That Shows Contrast

A Complete the following sentences about children in the United States using the words and phrases in the box.

differ from	major difference between	unlike
in contrast	significantly different from	

1 One _major difference between_ children in the United States in 1900 and now is that children in the past didn't get a lot of individual attention from their parents, while children today get a lot of individual attention.

2 Another way that today's children are __________ children in the past is that in the past, children often worked to help their families, but children now often work for their own extra spending money.

3 Today's children also __________ children in 1900 in that they are required to attend school.

4 Children in the past often had large families with several siblings. __________, many children today have one or two siblings or are only children.

5 In 1900, children were very independent. __________ them, children today depend on their parents a lot.

B Pair Work With a partner, draw a chart like the one below. Write five contrasting pieces of information about children in the 1900s and now in a culture that you are familiar with. Then present your information to the class, using vocabulary from A.

Children in the 1900s	Children Now

One major difference between young children in my native country today and in the 1900s is that in the 1900s, they used to work in factories. Today that's illegal.

74 Unit 5 Comparison and Contrast 1

---

5 Avoid Common Mistakes ⚠

1 Do not use *who* with inanimate nouns.

that

A study who showed the benefits of being an only child was published last year.

2 Do not omit the relative pronoun in subject relative clauses.

who

Children , have older siblings tend to be somewhat dependent.

3 Remember that the subject and the verb must agree in relative clauses.

have

Children who has siblings often become secure and confident adults.

4 Use *the same as*, not *the same than*.

as

Middle children often have the same level of creativity than youngest children.

Editing Task

Find and correct eight more mistakes in this body paragraph from an essay comparing trends in families in the past and today.

Families Past and Present

that

A major way that families have changed is the number of families have only one child. The number of families had only one child was low in the United States in the 1950s and 1960s. However, one-child families began increasing in the 1970s and are very common today. This is especially true in households who have only one parent.

5 One reason families are smaller is the cost of living. It is not the same than it was 40 years ago. For example, it costs about 10 times more to send a child to college than it did 40 years ago. As a result, many parents choose to have only one child because they do not have enough money for more children.

10 In addition, attitudes about only children are also not the same than attitudes about them in the past. In the 1950s and 1960s, people avoided having only one child. At that time, many people thought that children did not have siblings had many disadvantages. For example, people thought that they did not learn good social skills. However, recent studies who focus on only children show a different picture.

15 These studies show that only children tend to have the same social skills than children who has siblings.

Family Size and Personality 75

---

6 Academic Writing

In this section, you will write an outline and one body paragraph for a comparison and contrast essay using the block method. Before you start writing, you will learn how to write effective topic sentences.

About Topic Sentences

Topic sentences introduce the main idea of a body paragraph. In academic essays, they often appear at the beginning of body paragraphs. Although not all body paragraphs have topic sentences, it will help you to organize your writing if you always include one.

The following guidelines will help you write effective topic sentences:

1 An effective topic sentence should contain a claim or an opinion that needs to be supported with evidence. It should not be a fact that is widely accepted as true. Notice the difference in the following sentences:

- Some families are small. (a fact)
- Small families are better than large families. (a claim that needs to be supported with evidence)

2 The content of the topic sentences should relate back to the thesis statement of the essay.

- Siblings have different personality traits because of birth order. (thesis statement)
- Firstborn children are generally leaders. (topic sentence)

Organize Your Ideas

A For this assignment, you will use the block method of comparison and contrast for organizing your ideas.

Look at the block method outline for the essay on birth order below. Use the blank outline that follows to create an outline for your topic.

Title of Essay: Birth Order

Paragraph 1. Introductory paragraph. Thesis Statement: Experts agree that birth order tends to dictate some basic personality traits in children and adults.

Paragraph 2. Topic Sentence: Firstborn children often share several common traits.
• Traits: responsible, ambitious, authoritarian

Paragraph 3. Topic Sentence: Middle children exhibit unique characteristics.
• Traits: passive, solitary, realistic, creative, insightful

Paragraph 4. Topic Sentence: Youngest children have typical characteristics as well.
• Traits: dependent, controlling, creative, easygoing, social

Title of Essay: ______

Paragraph 1. Introductory paragraph. Thesis Statement: ______

Paragraph 2. Topic Sentence: ______

• **Details:** ______

Paragraph 3. Topic Sentence: ______

• **Details:** ______

Paragraph 4. Topic Sentence: ______

• **Details:** ______

B Pair Work Share your outline with a partner and discuss your ideas.

Writing Task

Write one of the body paragraphs from your outline. Follow the steps below.

1 Make sure that you have a clear topic sentence that follows the guidelines in About Topic Sentences on page 76.

2 Include the following in your paragraph:

- identifying relative clauses;
- as . . . as;
- common patterns that show contrast;
- at least three of these academic words from the essay in this unit: *adulthood, assumed, author, benefit, creative, environment, exhibit, expert, indicate, individual, insightful, intelligent, maintain, passive, research, role, unique.*

3 After you write your paragraph, review it and make sure that you avoided the mistakes in the Avoid Common Mistakes chart on page 75.

> **Academic Writing Tip**
> **Improving Your Internet Searches**
> When you do an Internet search, use quotation marks around important ideas. For example, "large families" will eliminate results with only "large" or "family" alone.

Peer Review

A Exchange your outline and paragraph with a partner. Answer the following questions as you read your partner's outline and work, and share your responses.

1 Is the outline organized using the block method?

2 Does the topic sentence relate to the thesis statement?

3 Are any identifying relative clauses, *as . . . as*, or common patterns that show contrast used in the paragraph?

4 Is anything confusing? Write a question mark (?) next to it.

5 Provide one compliment (something you found interesting or unusual).

B Use your partner's comments to help you revise your paragraph. Use the Writer's Checklist on page A2 to review your paragraph for organization, grammar, and vocabulary.

Kahoot!

for Grammar and Beyond
cambridge.org/kahoot/grammarandbeyond

What is Kahoot!?

Kahoot! is a game-based learning platform that makes it easy to create, share and play fun learning games and trivia quizzes in minutes. You can play Kahoot! on any mobile device or laptop with an internet connection.

What can you use kahoots for?

Kahoots can be used for review, formative assessment or homework.

When should you play Kahoot?

You can play kahoot quizzes before starting the unit as a diagnostic, during the unit as formative assessment, or at the end of a unit to test student knowledge.

To launch a live game in the classroom, find the kahoot for the level and unit and simply click on "play".

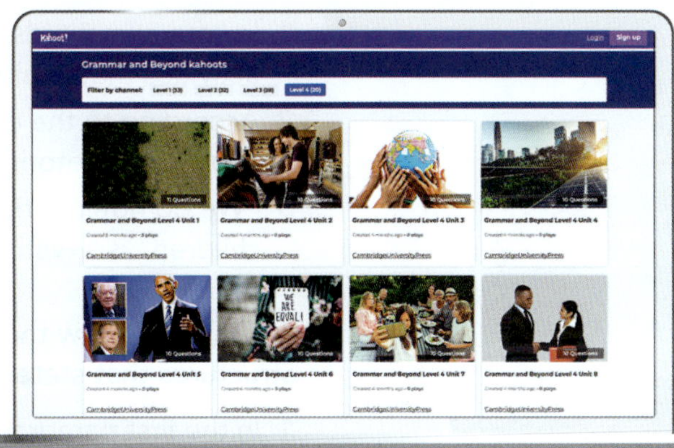

Quiz Your English app

Quiz Your English is a fun new way to practice, improve, and test your English by competing against learners from all around the world. Learn English grammar with friends, discover new English words, and test yourself in a truly global environment.

- Learn to avoid common mistakes with a special section just for *Grammar and Beyond* users
- Challenge your friends and players wherever they are
- Watch where you are on the leaderboards

Cause and Effect 1: Sentence Structure; Common Patterns with Nouns That Show Cause

The Environment and You

1 Grammar in the Real World

You will read an essay about ecological footprints, a measurement of the impact each person has on the world's natural resources. The essay is an example of one kind of cause and effect writing in which one cause leads to several effects.

A Before You Read What are three common things that people do in their everyday lives that have an impact on the environment? Read the essay. According to the writer, what might be one effect of mining for natural resources such as coal and oil?

B Comprehension Check Answer the questions.

1 In your own words, what is an ecological footprint? Provide examples of activities that could cause a large and a small ecological footprint.
2 According to the essay, what are three major consequences of large ecological footprints?
3 "We do not inherit the Earth from our ancestors; we borrow it from our children" is a Native American proverb. How is it related to the essay?

C Notice Follow the instructions below to help you notice sentence structures that state causes and describe effects.

1 In the first paragraph, find the sentence about easily accessible resources and large ecological footprints on lines 10–13. Write *C* above the clause that gives a reason or cause and *E* above the clause that states the effect. Circle the word that introduces the cause.
2 In the fourth paragraph, find the sentence that states the effect of releasing dangerous gases in the air. Circle the phrase that introduces the effect.
3 In the fourth paragraph, underline the first sentence. Does the sentence describe a cause or an effect? What phrase does the writer use to introduce it?

D Academic Writing Reread the introductory paragraph of the essay and underline the sentence that tells the reader the main idea. This sentence is called the *thesis statement*.

Ecological Footprints

Environmentalists are increasingly concerned about the impact that individuals have on our planet, and many people now want to help
5   protect the environment. A good place to start is reducing one's ecological footprint. An ecological footprint is an estimate of how much land, water, and other natural resources are being used by a person
10 or a group. Because resources are easily accessible in developed countries like the United States, people in these countries tend to have large ecological footprints. For example, they may take long showers,
15 leave their computers on for the whole day, buy new things they do not need, and fly frequently between cities. The consequences of large ecological footprints can be disastrous.[1]

20   One of the worst effects of large ecological footprints is the loss of natural resources, such as oil, water, and wood. These resources are being consumed so fast that the Earth does not have time to
25 renew them. Approximately 95 million barrels of oil are produced daily in the world (BP, 2019, p.16). People use oil to run their cars, heat their homes, and create products such as clothes, paint, and plastic.

30   Plastic is now one of the biggest threats to our environment, and in fact to each of us. The naturalist David Attenborough shocked the world by showing images of sea birds attempting to feed their young on
35 plastic shopping bags. It is estimated that eight million tons of plastic end up in our oceans every year (BBC, 2017). Unless this stops, there will be more plastic than fish in the ocean by 2050. Already, billions of
40 people around the world are drinking water that is contaminated by plastic. The United States is the country worst affected, with 94% plastic contamination in its tap water (Morrison & Tyree, 2017).

45   Large ecological footprints also lead to higher greenhouse gas emissions. The mining of oil, natural gas, and coal, as well as the use of these resources in electrical power plants and automobiles, releases dangerous
50 gases into the air, where they trap[2] heat. As a result, the Earth gets warmer.

It is our responsibility to find ways to decrease our impact on our planet. Even small changes can make a difference
55 and help to protect the environment. If we do not start reducing our ecological footprints right away, it may be too late for future generations to contain[3] the damage.

---

[1]**disastrous:** causing a lot of damage

[2]**trap:** prevent from leaving

[3]**contain:** limit

2 Sentence Structure: Simple and Compound Sentences

Grammar Presentation

In cause and effect writing and in academic writing in general, it is effective to use a variety of sentence types. Writers use simple sentences to express facts or opinions strongly. They use compound sentences to link related ideas such as causes and effects.

Simple sentence:
Lack of natural resources is one of the results of large ecological footprints.

Compound sentence:
Large ecological footprints cause many problems, and it is our social responsibility to solve them.

2.1 Simple Sentences

A A simple sentence has only one clause, called a *main clause* or an *independent clause.* Like all sentences, a simple sentence must have a subject and a verb.

> SUBJECT　　　　　　VERB
> *Millions of barrels of oil are produced daily.*

Many different elements may come after the verb, including:

object

> SUBJECT　　　　VERB　　　OBJECT
> *Plastic pollution has devastated **our oceans**.*

prepositional phrase

> SUBJECT　　　　　VERB　　　　PREP. PHRASE
> *Ozone and other greenhouse gases are often **in the news**.*

adjective

> SUBJECT　VERB　ADJECTIVE
> *The Earth is becoming **warmer**.*

adverb

> SUBJECT　　　　　　　　VERB　　ADVERB
> *Natural resources that provide energy will run out **eventually**.*

B The subject of a sentence must be a noun phrase. There are many different kinds of noun phrases, including:

adjective + noun

***Small changes** can make a difference.*

pronoun

***This** has devastated many oceans.*

noun and noun

***Ozone and other greenhouse gases** are often in the news.*

noun + prepositional phrase

***The health of our oceans** remains critical.*

noun + relative clause

***Natural resources that provide energy** will run out eventually.*

gerund

***Reducing our ecological footprints** is crucial.*

2.1 Simple Sentences *(continued)*

C The verb of a sentence can consist of a single main verb or a main verb with an auxiliary verb such as *be*, *do*, and *have*, or a modal such as *can* and *will*.

A verb phrase can consist of more than one verb.

MAIN VERB
*The health of our oceans **remains** critical.*

AUXILIARY VERB
*This **has** devastated many oceans.*

MODAL
*People **may** take long showers.*

*The average temperature **rises and falls**.*

2.2 Using Simple Sentences

A Use short simple sentences to emphasize an important point within the larger discourse.

The consequences of these footprints can be disastrous.

B If the subject or a verb is missing, the sentence is incomplete. It is called a *fragment*.

Avoid fragments by making sure all sentences have a subject and a verb.

FRAGMENT (MISSING SUBJECT): *In the future, will probably be much warmer on Earth.*

CORRECTION: *In the future, **the temperature** will probably be much warmer on Earth.*

FRAGMENT (MISSING VERB): *The worst effect of large ecological footprints the loss of natural resources.*

CORRECTION: *The worst effect of large ecological footprints **is** the loss of natural resources.*

C Academic writers connect independent clauses with transition words to make the relationship between two ideas very clear.

Some examples of transition words are:
as a result, consequently, furthermore, however

You can use a period or a semicolon before a transition word to connect the independent clauses. Use a comma after a transition word.

*These gases trap heat in the air. **As a result**, the Earth gets warmer.*

*These gases trap heat in the air; **as a result**, the Earth gets warmer.*

D You can connect two independent clauses with a semicolon. This is a good choice if the ideas in the two clauses are closely related.

INDEPENDENT CLAUSE 1   INDEPENDENT CLAUSE 2
People should buy less; they should replace items only when absolutely necessary.

A Use compound sentences to connect two ideas. A compound sentence includes at least two independent clauses that are connected by a coordinating conjunction (*and, but, or, so, yet*). Use a comma before the coordinating conjunction.

INDEPENDENT CLAUSE 1
Some people are concerned about the environment,

INDEPENDENT CLAUSE 2
so they recycle as much as they can.

B Avoid run-on sentences and comma splices. A run-on sentence is two independent clauses without a coordinating conjunction.

Use a comma and coordinating conjunction when connecting two independent clauses.

A comma splice is two independent clauses combined with a comma.

Use a period between the two independent clauses.

RUN-ON: *These gases trap heat in the air the Earth gets warmer.*

CORRECTION: *These gases trap heat in the air, **so** the Earth gets warmer.*

COMMA SPLICE: *Humans are the cause of many environmental problems, it is our responsibility to resolve them.*

CORRECTION: *Humans are the cause of many environmental problems. It is our responsibility to resolve them.*

C The use of *and* and *but* to introduce a sentence is common in some types of writing, such as in newspapers and magazines. However, it is not usually appropriate in academic writing.

*Natural resources are being consumed so fast that the Earth does not have time to renew them. **And** as a result, these resources are becoming scarce.*

*There are efforts to clean up the oceans. **But** the health of our oceans remains critical.*

Grammar Application

Exercise 2.1 Subjects and Verbs

Read about energy resources in Iceland. Underline the subject, and circle the verb in each independent clause.

1 Iceland has huge frozen glaciers, but it also has more than 100 volcanoes.

2 In 1998, Iceland decided to become independent from fossil fuels.

3 It began to increase its use of renewable energy sources.

4 Electricity in Iceland's homes is generated by geothermal springs, or it comes from the energy of the rivers and glaciers.

5 The water in geothermal springs is already hot, so Icelanders use it instead of fossil fuels to heat their homes.

6 Basic services such as transportation in Iceland are switching to electric vehicles, and all ships in the large fishing industry may eventually operate on hydrogen fuel.

7 Iceland satisfies its country's need for energy without relying heavily on fossil fuels.

Exercise 2.2 Fragments, Run-on Sentences, and Comma Splices

A Read the following sentences about the environment. Check (✓) each complete sentence. Write *F* for each fragment, *R-O* for each run-on, and *CS* for each comma splice.

1 (a) ___✓___ Over time, people have destroyed the natural habitats of many plants and animals in order to build more homes and grow more food. (b) ___*F*___ For this reason, many of our forests now gone. (c) ___*R-O*___ Plants and animals are losing their homes they may become extinct.

2 (a) _________ Water pollution a serious problem. (b) _________ For many years, people got rid of waste by dumping it into the water. (c) _________ As a result, the quality of the water in many of our oceans, rivers, and lakes unacceptable.
(d) _________ In fact, nearly about two billion people in the world do not have safe drinking water, and over two million people die each year from diseases related to water.

3 (a) _________ Environmentalists are constantly trying to come up with ideas to protect the environment nobody knows what the environment will be like in the future.
(b) _________ However, researchers believe that much has already improved.
(c) _________ Individuals are becoming more aware of the environment around them.

4 (a) _________ Trying to protect nature in various ways. (b) _________ Some people are helping to clean up the environment by driving electric cars, others are working to preserve endangered plants and animals. (c) _________ These efforts will allow future generations to have clean air and water and to enjoy the world's natural beauty.

5 (a) _________ The forests of the Earth are being cut down. (b) _________ The destruction of the forests is the result of human and natural disasters. (c) _________
Has negative consequences on the environment.

B Rewrite the fragments, run-ons, and comma splices in A. Use coordinating conjunctions, transition words, and punctuation to correct run-ons and comma splices. Check your answers with a partner.

1 *For this reason, many of our forests are now gone. Plants and animals are losing their homes. As a result, they may become extinct.*

2 ____

3 ____

4 ____

5 ____

3 Complex Sentences

Grammar Presentation

Another way to link cause and effect ideas is with complex sentences. Complex sentences have one independent clause and at least one dependent clause.

Because resources are readily accessible in developed countries like the United States, people in these countries tend to have large ecological footprints.

3.1 Complex Sentences

A complex sentence has an independent clause and a dependent clause introduced by a subordinator. Subordinators show the relationship between the two ideas.

Some examples of subordinators are: *although, after, as if, because, before, if, since, whereas, whether, while*

When the dependent clause comes first, use a comma to separate it from the independent clause.

INDEPENDENT CLAUSE
Future generations will suffer

DEPENDENT CLAUSE
if pollution is not reduced.

DEPENDENT CLAUSE
Although people try to save energy,

INDEPENDENT CLAUSE
global demand for energy increases every year.

3.2 Using Complex Sentences

A In academic writing, use complex sentences with the subordinators *because, if, since,* and *when* to express cause and effect relationships.

CAUSE   EFFECT
If pollution is reduced, global health will improve.

B A dependent clause that is not connected to an independent clause is a fragment.

Avoid dependent clause fragments in the following ways:

Connect the dependent clause to an independent clause. (Remember to use a comma after a dependent clause if it comes before an independent clause.)

OR

Change the subordinator to a transition word that can introduce an independent clause.

FRAGMENT: *Because energy use is high in the developed world. People there use a lot of resources.*

DEPENDENT CLAUSE
CORRECTION: *Because energy use is high in the*

INDEPENDENT CLAUSE
developed world, people there use a lot of resources.

CORRECTION: *Energy use is high in the developed world. As a result, people there use a lot of resources.*

Grammar Application

Exercise 3.1 Complex Sentences

A For each pair of sentences about bald eagles, write *C* next to the sentence that shows the cause and *E* next to the sentence that shows the effect. Next, combine the sentences using *because*, *if*, *since*, or *when*. Sometimes more than one answer is possible.

1. ___*E*___ The United States government declared bald eagles an endangered species.

   ___*C*___ Bald eagles were almost extinct in the 1960s.

   Because bald eagles were almost extinct in the 1960s, the United States government declared them an endangered species.

2. _______ The bald eagle showed the qualities of impressive strength and courage.

   _______ The bald eagle was chosen in 1782 to be the symbol for the United States.

3. _______ The government enacted laws that included banning the use of the pesticide DDT.

   _______ The bald eagle population began to recover.

4. _______ In 2007, the bald eagle was taken off the Endangered Species Act's "threatened" list.

   _______ The bald eagles' numbers had greatly increased since the 1960s.

5. _______ The bald eagle population may decrease once more.

   _______ The habitats of the bald eagles are not protected in the future.

6. _______ Some biologists are urging wind energy companies to develop safer turbines.

   _______ The birds are sometimes killed by the blades of wind turbines.

7. _______ People can help protect the bald eagle.

   _______ People volunteer to clean up the habitats where eagles nest.

B Pair Work With a partner, think of two endangered animals. Discuss why the animals are endangered (habitat loss, pesticides, overfishing, etc.) and what is being done to protect the animals. Next, do the role play below. Use *because*, *if*, *since*, and *when* where possible.

A You are a reporter. Interview Partner B about one of the animals you talked about. Ask why the animal is endangered and what the impact of environmental policies has been.

B You are an environmentalist. Answer Partner A's questions.

Partner A *Tell me about an endangered animal that people should know about.*

Partner B *Sea turtles are an endangered animal.*

Partner A *Why are they endangered?*

Partner B *One reason is the fishing industry. Many turtles die when they bite the hooks and get caught in the fishing lines.*

Partner A *How are they today?*

Partner B *Since there are now programs that protect the turtles, their numbers have improved in recent years.*

Switch roles and do the role play again using information about the second animal.

Read the questions below. Then listen to the radio interview about bikeshare programs in large cities. As you listen, take notes. Finally, answer the questions. Use *because*, *if*, *since*, and *when*.

1 Why are bikeshares becoming so popular in large cities?

Bikeshares are becoming popular because they are a great way to reduce pollution.

2 Why do people use a bikeshare?

3 What do people have to do if they want to use the bikes?

4 What happens when riders get a flat tire?

5 If a city wants a bikeshare program to be successful, what two things are required?

6 What can bikeshare riders do in some cities when they want to find a bike or an empty space at a station?

7 Why do some people feel uncomfortable riding the bikes?

4 Common Patterns with Nouns That Show Cause 🌐

Vocabulary Presentation

<table>
<tr>
<td>Cause and effect relationships can be shown in many different ways. One important way is through the use of the nouns cause, reason, and factor.</td>
<td>One important cause of overpopulation is lack of education.
Low cost is the primary reason why many communities use coal for energy.
Emissions from cars are a major factor in the increase in air pollution.</td>
</tr>
</table>

4.1 Nouns That Show Cause: *Cause, Reason, Factor*

A The following expressions and patterns are commonly used with the noun *cause* and a form of the verb *be*:

NOUN PHRASE   NOUN PHRASE
_________ *is a/one cause of* _________.

NOUN PHRASE   NOUN PHRASE
Another cause of _________ *is* _________.

*A higher birth rate **is one** major **cause of** overpopulation.*

Another *leading **cause of** overpopulation **is** the decline in death rates.*

B Expressions with cause generally describe a negative effect. *Cause* does not usually occur with words that are related to success or positive results.

*Some researchers believe that the primary cause of **global warming** is large ecological footprints.*

C These expressions and patterns are commonly used with the noun *reason* a form of the verb *be*:

CLAUSE   CLAUSE
One reason (why) ______ is ______.

CLAUSE   NOUN PHRASE
One reason (why) ______ is ______.

NOUN PHRASE   CLAUSE
The reason for ______ is ______.

NOUN PHRASE   NOUN PHRASE
The reason for ______ is ______.

SENTENCE
______. For this reason / these

CLAUSE
reasons, ______.

One reason (why) the population **is** growing so fast **is** that death rates have fallen dramatically.

One reason (why) the population is growing so fast **is** the decline in the death rate.

The real **reason for** our concern about overpopulation **is** that our resources are limited.

The primary **reason for** our concern about overpopulation **is** limited resources.

People are living longer, healthier lives. **For this reason,** the population has been increasing.

D These expressions and patterns are commonly used with the noun *factor* and a form of the verb *be*:

NOUN PHRASE   NOUN PHRASE
______ is a / one factor in ______.

NOUN PHRASE   NOUN PHRASE
Another factor in ______ is ______.

Mortality **is one** key **factor in** the current growth in population.

Another critical **factor in** water pollution **is** the increase in fertilizer use by farmers.

🌐 DATA FROM THE REAL WORLD

Adjectives that most frequently occur with *cause* are: leading, probable, common, root, underlying, exact, major, likely, main, important, primary	Scholars are not sure whether poverty is an **underlying cause** of overpopulation.
Adjectives that most frequently occur with *reason* are: good, major, real, main, primary, biggest	One **good reason** to recycle is to save money.
Adjectives that most frequently occur with *factor* are: important, another, major, key, significant, critical	Decreasing the number of cars on the road is a **critical factor** in the effort to reduce air pollution.

Vocabulary Application

A Complete the online article about ways to get around. Use *cause*, *reason*, or *factor* and appropriate adjectives from the Data from the Real World box above.

Changing with the Times

Some experts say that one ___*leading cause*___ of air pollution is the carbon emissions from
(1)

cars. To reduce these emissions, many people have changed how they get around. James Kendall

of Cincinnati, Ohio, sold his gas-guzzling car and purchased a hybrid vehicle. Kendall says,

"One ___________________ ___________________ I bought a hybrid is that it's better for the
(2)

environment. However, another ___________________ ___________________ in my decision was
(3)

money. I spend a lot less on gas now."

Linda Wong of Los Angeles, California, takes public transportation as often as she can. "Carbon

emissions from cars is the ___________________ ___________________ of smog and air pollution
(4)

in L.A.," she explains. "I don't want to add to that. That's the ___________________ why I don't
(5)

like to drive. Another ___________________ ___________________ in my decision is that driving
(6)

in L.A. is very stressful."

Pedro Sandoval of Missoula, Montana, started using a carpool to get to and from work two

years ago because of his concern for the environment, but he says that the ___________________
(7)

___________________ that he has stuck with it has to do with other incentives. "I've met a lot

of really nice people and saved a lot of money." He'll take public transportation, but, as he says,

buses are a ___________________ of pollution, too.
(8)

B Pair Work With a partner, choose three environmentally related issues. Below are some
ideas. Explain possible causes and effects for each one using expressions with *factor*, *reason*,
and *cause*.

noise pollution	nuclear safety	overpopulation	water pollution

*The use of medicines is a factor in water pollution. The medicines we use end up
in our water. For this reason, some communities have started to collect unused
medicines so that they don't end up in our water.*

A Answer the questions about ways that people and cities are lessening their impact on the environment. Use expressions and patterns with *cause*, *reason*, or *factor*, and adjectives from Data from the Real World.

1 What is one reason why some people prefer not to eat meat?

One primary reason why some people prefer not to eat meat is that they don't want animals to be killed for food.

2 What do you think is one reason for the rising interest in locally grown food?

3 What are two causes of pollution in cities?

4 What is one important factor in a city's decision to start a bikeshare program?

5 Some cities have decided to ban the use of plastic bags in grocery stores. What do you think is the reason for this ban?

B Pair Work With a partner, take turns asking and answering the questions in A. Do you agree or disagree with each other's answers? Tell why.

I disagree that people don't eat meat because they don't want animals to be killed.
I think that some people don't eat meat because they can't afford it.

5 Avoid Common Mistakes  

1 Avoid fragments. Make sure sentences have a subject and a verb.

The result of a large ecological footprint ^is often pollution.

2 Use *because*, not *cuz* or *coz*, in written academic English.

Animals are becoming extinct ~~cuz~~ because humans have moved into their habitats.

3 Do not confuse *cause* with *because*.

~~Cause~~ Because water pollution is widespread, there is a shortage of clean drinking water in many parts of the world.

4 Avoid beginning sentences with *and* in written academic English.

Shoppers should bring their own bags to stores because paper bags lead to ~~deforestation. And~~ deforestation, and plastic bags are dangerous for birds and marine life.

Editing Task

Find and correct eight more mistakes in this paragraph from an essay about ocean pollution.

One significant cause of ocean pollution *is* the accidental spilling of crude oil by large ocean-going ships. The consequences of oil spills can be disastrous to both plant and animal marine life. For example, oil that spills on the surface of the water blocks oxygen from getting to marine plant life. Cause oxygen is necessary for
5 survival, marine plants die. And the fish that eat them can die as well. In addition, oil spills can coat the feathers of marine birds. Oil-coated birds can become weighted down, so cannot fly. Furthermore, oil often removes the natural coating on marine birds' feathers. As a result, the birds can die from overexposure cuz the coating protects them from the elements. Oil spills also affect the human food chain.
10 This occurs coz shellfish such as mussels and clams filter water through their bodies. If the water is polluted with oil, the flesh of the shellfish becomes polluted as well. And this makes them harmful for human consumption. Cause oil spills affect human, animal, and plant life, many people agree that these spills one of the most serious environmental problems in the world today.

6 Academic Writing

In this section, you will write an introductory paragraph for a cause and effect essay that describes one cause leading to several effects. Before you start writing, you will learn how to write effective thesis statements.

About Thesis Statements

The introductory paragraph of an essay has three parts: the hook, which introduces the topic; additional background information on the topic; and a thesis statement. A thesis statement states the main idea of the essay and gives a preview of what the writer is going to say about the topic. It usually comes at the end of the paragraph.

There are two types of thesis statements:

1 **General thesis statements** A general thesis statement tells the reader the topic of the essay, but not the exact points that will be made. The specific points will appear later in the topic sentences of the body paragraphs.

NON-SPECIFIC IDEAS

*There are **three main reasons** for not driving a car to help build a better future.*

NON-SPECIFIC IDEAS

*Drastic lifestyle changes will have both **positive and negative effects**.*

2 Specific thesis statements A specific thesis statement tells the reader the exact arguments or points that will be developed in the essay. Usually, the points are listed in the same order in which they appear in the body paragraphs.

SPECIFIC ARGUMENTS

*Becoming a strict vegetarian can lead to **a healthier body, a smaller ecological footprint, and a more spiritual life**.*

SPECIFIC POINTS

*Some ways to lead a healthy life include **waking up early, exercising, and meditating**.*

Exercise

A Read the thesis statements below. Label each one as general (*G*) or specific (*S*).

1 _______ A dramatic increase in population will cause several major environmental changes.

2 _______ Environmental policies can reduce air pollution, traffic congestion, and water use.

3 _______ "Green" office buildings will lead to cleaner air, lower costs, and healthier workers.

4 _______ Neighborhood groups can improve the environment in several important ways.

B Imagine that each thesis statement in A was in the introduction to an essay. Match each statement below to a thesis statement in A. Write the number (1, 2, 3, 4) on the line.

a _______ People can start community gardens that provide fresh local produce.

b _______ Installing solar panels in buildings could reduce heat and electricity costs.

c _______ Water resources may become scarce.

d _______ Raising the tax on gasoline will discourage people from driving.

Pre-writing Tasks
Choose a Topic

A Choose one of the essay topics listed below. You will write an introductory paragraph for a cause and effect essay on this topic. This essay will describe one cause (your topic) leading to several effects.

- The impact of overpopulation on the environment
- Lifestyle changes that can decrease one's ecological footprint
- A topic of your own approved by your teacher

B Pair Work Write a list of effects that you might include in an essay on this topic. Choose three major effects. Then share your ideas with a partner.

Organize Your Ideas

A Draw a chart like the one below on a separate sheet of paper, and complete it to organize your ideas.

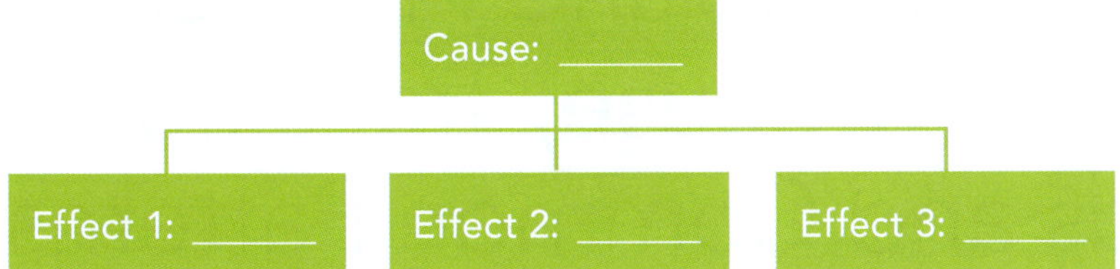

B Pair Work Explain your chart to your partner, and discuss how you will organize your introductory paragraph.

Writing Task

Write an introductory paragraph. Follow the steps below.

1 Use the information from your chart in Organize Your Ideas to write your introductory paragraph. Your thesis statement should state the cause and three effects.

2 Include the following in your paragraph:
- variety of sentence types: simple, compound, and complex;

> **Academic Writing Tip**
>
> **Avoid Fragments with *Because***
>
> Remember to connect *because* to an independent clause.
>
> *People buy locally produced food because it is in their long-term interest.*

- at least one of the phrases that you learned with *cause*, *reason*, and *factor*;
- at least three of these academic words from the essay in this unit: *accessible*, *consequences*, *consume*, *consumption*, *create*, *environment*, *environmentalist*, *estimate*, *generation*, *impact*, *individual*, *item*, *release*, *resource*.

3 After you write your introductory paragraph, review it and make sure you avoided the mistakes in the Avoid Common Mistakes chart on page 14.

Peer Review

A Exchange your paragraph with a partner. Answer the following questions as you read your partner's paragraph, and then share your responses.

1 What is the topic?

2 What is the thesis statement? Is the thesis statement general or specific? Underline it.

3 What are the cause and effects that will be addressed in the essay?

4 Are all the sentences complete? Are there any fragments, run-ons, or comma splices?

5 Does the paragraph contain a variety of sentence types and transition words?

6 Is anything confusing? Write a question mark (?) next to it.

7 Provide one compliment (something you found interesting or unusual).

B Use your partner's comments to help you revise your paragraph. Use the Writer's Checklist on page A2 to review your paragraph for organization, grammar, and vocabulary.

Cause and Effect 2: Subordinators and Prepositions That Show Cause; Transition Words and Common Patterns with Nouns That Show Effect

Consumer Behavior

1 Grammar in the Real World

You will read an essay about the factors that influence consumers' buying behavior. The essay is an example of one type of cause and effect writing in which several causes lead to one effect.

A Before You Read What is the biggest purchase you made in the past six months? What influenced you in making your decision? Read the essay. What does the writer state are the key factors that affect consumer buying behavior?

B Comprehension Check Answer the questions.

1 According to the text, what is the definition of consumer behavior? Use your own words.

2 Name one factor from the essay that might influence someone to buy more and one factor from the essay that might influence someone to buy less.

3 Why is it important to understand consumer behavior?

C Notice Follow the instructions below to help you notice the words the writer uses to state causes and describe effects.

1 Find the word *effect* in the first paragraph and circle it. Underline the verb, adjective, and preposition that combine with the word *effect*. Notice how the author uses the word *effect* twice in the fifth paragraph with different adjectives. Underline the phrases with *effect* and circle the adjectives.

2 Find the sentence in the second paragraph that describes a possible effect of being hungry when one shops. Circle the words that introduce the result in the sentence that follows it.

D Academic Writing What type of opening sentence does the writer use to attract the reader's attention?

a definition   b interesting fact   c provocative question

Understanding
Consumer Behavior

Consumer behavior is the process consumers go through in making purchasing decisions. This process includes the steps they take from the moment they become aware of a
5 particular need through the final decision to purchase or not purchase a product. According to marketing experts, this process includes the time spent planning where to shop and comparison shopping. Along the way, consumers
10 are influenced by many factors, including psychological and physical ones. Many experts agree on four factors that have a significant effect on consumer behavior.

One set of factors that influence consumer
15 behavior is physical factors – how a person physically feels when shopping. For example, being hungry when grocery shopping affects how people shop. The result is that people often buy more food than they would if they were not
20 hungry. In contrast, feeling tired leads people to buy less.

Cultural and social factors also have an effect on consumer behavior. Some people make choices because of what their friends do. One
25 example is the importance attached to owning a particular item, such as an expensive pair of jeans, in a person's social network. Another social factor is whether the culture encourages or discourages a behavior, such as bargaining for a lower price.

30 A third factor that impacts consumer behavior is a person's self-image. People often try to match their purchases, from paper towels to cars, to their idea of self. For example, some people care very much about the environment and health
35 of the planet. Therefore, they might choose to drive an electric car due to its low impact on the environment. Other people might see themselves as economical shoppers. As a result, they might buy only simple, inexpensive clothing in order to
40 maintain that aspect of their self-image.

Finally, a person's own experience is a factor. Memories about a certain product or place can have a direct effect on later decisions. For instance, people will tend to go back to
45 a restaurant because they had a good eating experience there. On the other hand, if a person becomes ill eating seafood, it might have a negative effect on his or her future desire for that kind of food.

50 Every day, people make choices about what to buy. However, they are often unaware of the process behind their decision making. As a result, they can become vulnerable to[1] advertising and other marketing techniques that target the factors
55 that convince people to buy more. Consumers may want to make changes in their purchasing patterns, but they might not know how to make these changes. One important step is for them to become more aware of why they make choices.
60 Becoming educated about their behavior as consumers is an important way for people to make better buying decisions.

---

[1] **vulnerable to:** able to be easily hurt or influenced

2 Subordinators and Prepositions That Show Cause, Reason, or Purpose

Grammar Presentation

Some subordinators and prepositions show cause, reason, or purpose in academic writing. They answer the question *why*. Both subordinators and prepositions may be a word or a phrase.

*Some people buy products they do not need only **because** they are on sale.*

*We often choose what products to buy **as a result of** past experience.*

2.1 Using Subordinators That Show Cause, Reason, or Purpose

A Subordinators connect dependent clauses to independent clauses. These dependent clauses are adverb clauses.

INDEPENDENT CLAUSE
Some consumers purchase certain products
DEPENDENT CLAUSE
***because** they want to maintain their self-image.*

B As taught in Unit 1, use the subordinators *because* and *since* to indicate the cause or reason.

EFFECT   CAUSE / REASON
*Some consumers buy products **because** they want to be like their friends.*

C Use the following subordinators to indicate purpose:

so / so that

PURPOSE
*Some consumers buy "green" products **so (that)** they can appear environmentally aware.*

2.2 Using Prepositions That Show Cause or Reason

Use the following prepositions to indicate cause or reason. Unlike subordinators, they are followed by noun phrases:

because of, as a result of, due to

EFFECT   CAUSE / REASON
*Some people choose products **because of** their past experiences.*

EFFECT   CAUSE / REASON
*Shoppers will buy more food **as a result of** being hungry when they shop.*

EFFECT   CAUSE / REASON
*Some consumers choose an electric car **due to** its low impact on the environment.*

Grammar Application

Exercise 2.1 Subordinators That Show Cause, Reason, or Purpose

A In each pair of clauses about consumer behavior, write *C* above the clause that states a cause and *E* above the clause that states an effect. Next, combine the clauses using the words in parentheses. Sometimes more than one answer is possible.

           C   *E*

1. our decisions affect our financial future / it is important for us to make responsible buying decisions (*because*) *It is important for us to make responsible buying decisions because they affect our financial future.*

2. it is not easy to ignore advertising / consumers need to learn how to shop wisely (*since*)

3. make a list before you leave home / you do not buy something you do not need (*so that*)

4. people can get into debt easily / it is easy to buy things using a credit card (*because*)

5. children see the snack foods and ask their parents for them / stores put snack foods on low shelves (*so that*)

6. people will impulsively buy products that they don't need / stores put fun items like candy and toys by the checkout counters (*so*)

B Group Work Complete the sentences with your own ideas on a separate sheet of paper. Then share your sentences with your group and explain them. Ask your classmates if they agree or disagree with your ideas and tell why.

1. Sometimes people buy things they don't need because . . .
2. Sometimes people spend more money than they make because . . .
3. Manufacturers of cereals often include cartoon characters in their commercials so . . .
4. Fast-food restaurants often air commercials during late-night TV so that . . .
5. Stores sometimes advertise a few items at very low prices because . . .
6. Some people prefer to buy products online since . . .

A *My sentence is* People buy things they don't need because they want to feel better. *For example, when I have a bad day, sometimes I go out and buy something – even something small like a book – to make myself feel better.*

B *I agree with you because I do that, too, but I think more often people buy things they don't need because they are bored.*

Complete the sentences about consumer buying habits. The subordinators and prepositions are missing one word each. Write the missing word.

Consumers buy things for a lot of different reasons. Most frequently, people buy products _____*because*_____ of their individual tastes. For example, they might buy
(1)
the same snacks or cereals every time they go shopping _______________ to their
(2)
family's likes and dislikes. They don't even think about whether or not they want those items. People also make purchases as a _______________ of need. They buy an air
(3)
conditioner _______________ of severe hot weather, or they purchase fire alarms
(4)
in their house _______________ that their family stays safe. Finally, sometimes
(5)
people make impulse purchases. They buy things they haven't planned to buy and may not necessarily need or even want. Sometimes they make these purchases
_______________ a result of effective advertising or in the case of food, because
(6)
_______________ hunger while they are shopping. They also make impulse
(7)
purchases due _______________ their own personalities. Some people are more
(8)
prone to impulse buying than others are.

A You will listen to an interview about a person's buying habits. First read the questions. Then listen and take notes on the answers. Finally, write answers to the questions using sentences with the words in parentheses.

1 Why does Roger sometimes go shopping when he doesn't need anything?

(because) *He goes shopping when he doesn't need anything because he's happy when he is shopping.*

2 How does he control his spending?

(so that) ____

____

3 Does he use a credit card or debit card for his purchases? Why or why not?

(because of) ____

____

4 Why does he do a lot of research when he has to buy an expensive product?

(as a result of) ____

____

5 Does he eat out a lot?

(*due to*) ____

B Pair Work Rewrite questions 2–5 in A to interview your partner. On a separate sheet of paper, write sentences with his or her answers. Try to use the same prepositions and subordinating conjunctions. Share your sentences with another pair. How similar are your habits and experiences?

3 Transition Words and Phrases That Show Effect

Grammar Presentation

Another important way to link cause and effect in academic writing is with transition words and phrases. Transition words often signal a cause, a reason, or an effect.

*Sometimes people buy products that show that they are part of a social network. **Therefore,** they might choose an expensive pair of jeans because the jeans are popular with their friends.*

3.1 Using Transition Words and Phrases That Show Effect

A Transition words and phrases connect two independent clauses.

Separate the clauses with a semicolon or use two separate sentences.

Use a comma after the transition word or phrase.

*Environmental values might affect some purchases; **consequently,** many merchants offer green products.*

*Environmental values might affect some purchases. **Consequently,** many merchants offer green products.*

B The following transition words and phrases are used to show effect or result:

as a consequence, as a result, consequently, therefore, thus

Note: Thus is rarely used in informal speech or informal writing.

*Many consumers are concerned about the environment. **As a result,** they buy products that are environmentally safe.*

*Some consumers feel the need to be part of a certain group; **therefore,** they buy products that are expensive and fashionable.*

Grammar Application

A Unscramble the sentences about the effects of advertisements on consumers, using the prompts in parentheses. Remember to use a comma after the transition words and phrases.

1 People see and hear over 2,500 advertisements per day.

   As a result, people need to be aware of the effects of advertising.
   (of advertising / be / people / need to / aware of / the effects / as a result)

2 Candy and sugary cereals are advertised during children's television shows.

   ____
   (for them / a desire / children / develop / as a consequence)

3 Public television does not show advertisements for sugary foods.

   ____
   (exposed to / not / children / are / them / as a result)

4 The effects of smoking are serious and possibly deadly.

   ____
   (it / not / on TV / them / legal / to advertise / is / therefore)

5 Happy people are often shown eating snack foods.

   ____
   (think / them / viewers / too / snack foods / happy / will make / eating / consequently)

B Pair Work With a partner, choose two different products. How is each product advertised? What effects do you think the advertisements have on consumers? On a separate sheet of paper, write five sentences about each product using the cause and effect words in A. Then share your ideas with another pair of students.

The first product we discussed was an exercise shoe. Every ad shows young, thin women who are very pretty wearing the shoes. They have handsome boyfriends, and they seem very happy. Consequently, when I see the advertisements, I always think I should buy the shoes.

A Match the causes and effects of advertising techniques and their influence on consumers' buying decisions.

Causes	Effects	
1 Advertisements equate high prices with effectiveness.	*1* a	Consumers end up buying expensive brands.
2 Some advertisements target children.	b	Consumers buy more than they need.
3 Prices for large quantities of food are discounted.	c	Consumers sometimes buy products that might not be good for them.
4 Advertisements often show beautiful people.	d	Children start to become consumers early.
5 Sometimes ads do not focus on the ill effects of the products.	e	Consumers believe the products will make them beautiful, too.

B Combine each pair of causes and effects in A. Write sentences using *as a consequence, as a result, consequently,* and *therefore.* Use each transition word or phrase once.

1 *Advertisements equate high prices with effectiveness. As a result, consumers end up buying more expensive brands.*

2

3

4

5

C Group Work Discuss recent purchases that your group has made. What factors influenced you in your buying decision? Write five sentences based on the answers from your group using transition words and phrases such as *as a consequence, as a result, for this reason,* and *therefore.* Share the information with another group of students.

A friend of Amy's daughter had her ears pierced recently. For this reason, Amy's daughter wanted to get her ears pierced, too.
Julia Rozzio watched a very funny commercial about electric cars. As a result, when it was time to buy a new car, she decided to buy an electric one.

4 Common Patterns with Nouns That Show Effect

Vocabulary Presentation

There are several common expressions with the nouns *effect* and *result* that are used to show effect in cause and effect writing.

Advertising **can have a big effect on** children and teens.

The increase in sales **is a direct result of** our ad campaign.

4.1 Expressions with *Effect* and *Result*

A Some common expressions and patterns with the noun *effect* are:

| NOUN PHRASE | NOUN PHRASE |

The / One effect of __________ on __________ is

NOUN PHRASE

__________ .

NOUN PHRASE · · · NOUN PHRASE

__________ have an effect on __________ .

One effect of advertising **on** the public **is** overconsumption.

Advertising **can have a** significant **effect on** children and teens.

B Some common expressions and patterns with the noun *result* are:

NOUN PHRASE · · · NOUN PHRASE

__________ is a result of __________ .

CLAUSE · · · NOUN PHRASE

When / If __________ , the result is __________ .

NOUN PHRASE

__________ have a result.

Overconsumption **is a** predictable **result of** consumers' unawareness of sophisticated advertising techniques.

When / If consumers are unaware of their behavior, **the** primary **result may be** overconsumption.

Consumer awareness of advertising techniques often **has a** positive **result**.

⊕ DATA FROM THE REAL WORLD

Adjectives that most frequently occur with effect are:
no, little, significant, some

Research suggests that advertising has **little effect** on a family's food budget.

Adjectives that most frequently occur with result are:
direct, positive, predictable, primary

Women's desire to be thin is a **direct result** of advertising.

Vocabulary Application

Exercise 4.1 Common Patterns with Nouns That Show Effect

A Complete the following paragraph about the consumer behavior of working parents using the phrases in the box. Add appropriate punctuation as needed.

a direct result can be	one effect of	effect on
a positive effect on	effect of	~~have a significant effect on~~

These days, both parents work full-time in many families. This fact can **_have a significant effect on_** (1) their consumer behavior. In general, too, the behavioral change will have ___________________ (2) the economy. Parents with full-time jobs may not have time to cook dinner when they get home from work. As a result, they may spend more money in restaurants than families with non-working parents do. Dual-income families may eat out a lot or bring prepared food home. Some parents who work full-time may want to spend a lot of time with their children when they are not working. ___________________ (3) that they do special activities with their children that cost money. For example, they might take their children to amusement parks or go to the movies with them on the weekends. Some parents may also have to wear business attire for their jobs, which has an ___________________ (4) their clothing expenses. Another ___________________ (5) a dual-income lifestyle may be higher commuting expenses. The working parents may have two cars or pay twice the amount in public transportation costs. In sum, ___________________ (6) a dual-income lifestyle is that it will benefit the economy.

B Pair Work Write answers to the questions about the consumer behavior of parents below. Then share your answers with a partner. Use the common patterns with nouns to show effect with an appropriate adjective in each sentence.

1   How does having two working parents in a family affect the family's consumer behavior?

   One positive effect of working parents on children is that the children
   need to become more responsible.

2   How does the fact that working parents may not have time to cook dinner affect their lives?

3   What effect can having a dual income have on entertainment expenses?

4   How might working parents' jobs affect a family's clothing expenses?

5   How does a dual-income lifestyle affect a family's commuting expenses?

Exercise 4.2 More Common Patterns with Nouns That Show Effect

A Answer the questions about consumer behavior. Use the expressions with *effect* and *result* and adjectives from Data from the Real World where appropriate in your answers.

1   Some stores, especially clothing stores, play loud music. If a store plays loud music, does the store have a positive or negative effect on you? Why? Would you walk into the store or not?

   Music always has a positive effect on me. If I like the music, then
   I'll go into the store.

2   Do brand names have a significant effect on your decision to buy clothes? Why or why not?

3   Why do some people prefer to buy expensive brands? What is it a direct result of? Explain your opinion.

4   What do you think the primary result of advertising is on young children?

5   What kind of effect do consumer reviews on websites have on you as a consumer?

6   Why are some people thrifty? What could it be the result of?

B Group Work Share your answers in a group. Decide on answers to each question that you all agree on. Share them with the class.

5 Avoid Common Mistakes ⚠ 

1 Do not confuse *affect* and *effect*. *Affect* is almost always a verb; *effect* is almost always a noun.

Product placement in movies usually has a strong ~~affect~~ **effect** *on sales.*

2 Remember to use the correct preposition in expressions with *cause, result,* and *effect.*

Cartoon characters in ads have a significant effect ~~in~~ **on** *children.*

As a result ~~of~~ **of** *advertising on Saturday mornings, the company reached their target market – children.*

3 Do not confuse *because* with *because of*. Follow *because* with a subject and verb; follow *because of* with a noun.

Advertisers are coming up with new ways to market products because ~~of~~ young consumers are paying less attention to ads.

Advertisers are coming up with new ways to market products because **of** *young people's disinterest in ads.*

Editing Task

Find and correct six more mistakes in this body paragraph from an essay about effective advertising campaigns.

Overexposure to advertising has gradually resulted ~~on~~ **in** consumer inattention. In fact, studies have shown that most advertisements have little affect in consumers. One way in which manufacturers are responding to this problem is by a technique known as product placement. Rather than spending money on advertisements that consumers ignore, companies place their products in TV shows or films. For example,

5   characters drink a particular brand of soda, drive a particular type of car, or use a certain computer. An example of successful product placement is the use of Apple products in various TV shows and films. In 2010, Apple's products were present in 30 percent of that year's top 33 films. This resulted on increased sales for Apple because product placement. Product placement has a second beneficial affect.

10   Placing products in movies and TV shows, allows film companies to lower production costs because of they can use products for free. For example, the TV show *My Fair Wedding* features several jewelry and makeup brands in each episode. Without product placement, producers might have to purchase the jewelry and makeup. As a result on using product placement, the show's producers use the jewelry and makeup

15   for free.

6 Academic Writing

In this section, you will write an introductory paragraph for a cause and effect essay. Before you start writing, you will learn how to write engaging hooks.

About Hooks

Writers create interest and motivate readers to keep reading by including a "hook" in the introductory paragraph of an essay. The hook is usually the first or second sentence of the paragraph.

The following are four types of hooks:

1 **An unusual or surprising fact**

   Essay Topic: Overconsumption in the United States

   Hook: *Americans use 67 million tons of paper annually, or almost 850 million trees (U.S. EPA, 2019).*

2 **A definition of a key term or concept**

   Essay Topic: Consumer behavior

   Hook: *Consumer behavior is the process consumers go through in making purchasing decisions. This·process includes the steps one takes from the moment he or she becomes aware of a particular need through the final decision to purchase or not purchase a product (Perner, 2008).*

3 **A thought-provoking question**

   Essay Topic: What the government can do to prevent negative effects of advertisements on children

   Hook: *Should the government prohibit all advertisements on children's TV programs?*

4 **A quotation**

   Essay Topic: The effects of overconsumption

   Hook: *"Too many people spend money they haven't earned, to buy things they don't want, to impress people they don't like" (Will Rogers, American humorist).*

Exercise

A Match the examples of hooks below to the types of hooks in the box.

definition of a key term	thought-provoking question
quotation	unusual or surprising fact

1 Should the government have the power to stop parents from smoking in their own homes?
   thought-provoking question

2 "There are two ways to get enough: one is to continue to accumulate more and more. The other is to desire less" (G. K. Chesterton, 1874–1936). _______________

3 Every ton of recycled office paper saves 380 gallons of oil. _______________

4 Many people define advertising as the marketing and promotion of a product. _______________

5 Glass produced from recycled glass instead of raw materials reduces related air pollution by 20 percent, and water pollution by 50 percent. _______________

B Group Work In a small group, read the following thesis statements, and discuss possible hooks that could begin an essay containing each one. Share your ideas with another group.

1 Three main factors in childhood determine how people approach eating throughout their lives.
2 In order to stick to a budget, consumers need to address both internal and external forces before and during shopping.
3 Traffic jams can be the result of accidents, bad weather, and a lack of public transportation.

Pre-writing Tasks
Choose a Topic

A Choose one of the essay topics listed below. You will write an introductory paragraph for a cause and effect essay on this topic. This essay will describe many causes leading to one effect.

- Factors that influence your buying behavior
- Social and cultural influences on behavior
- A topic of your own approved by your teacher

B Pair Work Share your topic with a partner. Describe the multiple causes and the one effect you are going to write about. Give each other suggestions about ideas or facts to include.

A Use the chart below to organize your ideas.

	Factors/Causes	Effect
1		
2		
3		
4		
5		

B Group Work In a small group, share your completed chart and discuss these questions: Are all the causes clear? Are any important causes missing? Then modify your chart following the discussion.

Writing Task

Write an introductory paragraph. Follow the steps below.

1 Use the information in your chart in Organize Your Ideas to write a thesis statement. The thesis statement should include several causes and one effect that you are going to describe.

2 Write a hook that will work well for your topic. Use the description and examples in About Hooks to help you.

3 Include the following in your paragraph:

- subordinating conjunctions and transition words and phrases to link the ideas in your paragraph;

- common patterns with the nouns *effect* and *result* to show effect;

- at least three of these academic words from the essay in this unit: *affect, aspect, attached, aware, consumer, convince, culture, economical, environment, expert, factor, final, finally, image, impact, item, maintain, negative, network, physical, physically, process, psychological, purchase, significant, target, technique, unaware.*

4 After you write your introductory paragraph, review it and make sure you avoided the mistakes in the Avoid Common Mistakes chart on page 29.

Peer Review

A Exchange your paragraph with a partner. Answer the following questions as you read your partner's paragraph, and then share your responses.

1 What is the thesis statement? Underline it.

2 Is the hook interesting and effective? Why? Which of the four kinds of hooks was used?

3 What are the several causes and one effect that will be addressed in the essay?

4 What subordinating conjunctions and transition words did your partner use in the paragraph?

5 Is anything confusing? Write a question mark (?) next to it.

6 Provide one compliment (something you found interesting or unusual).

B Use your partner's comments to help you revise your paragraph. Use the Writer's Checklist on page A2 to review your paragraph for organization, grammar, and vocabulary.

3

Cause and Effect 3: Real and Unreal Conditionals; Common Phrases with *If* and *Unless*

Social Responsibility

1 Grammar in the Real World

You will read an essay that describes what might happen if corporations were to make socially responsible decisions. The essay is another example of cause and effect writing in which one cause leads to several effects.

A Before You Read What do you think it means for a company to act in a socially responsible manner? What can companies do to help local communities? Read the essay. According to the writer, what are the benefits of companies being socially responsible?

B Comprehension Check Answer the questions.

1 How can corporate social responsibility benefit the community?

2 Why does the writer argue that it is important that companies implement green policies?

3 Explain this sentence in the last paragraph: "Supporters say that it is not just that a company makes money, but *how* it makes money."

C Notice Follow the instructions below to help you notice sentence structures that state causes and describe effects.

1 Find a sentence in the first paragraph that contains an *if* clause. This sentence contains ideas that express cause and effect. Does the *if* clause or the main clause state the effect (result)? How certain is the writer of this effect? What word in the main clause gives the certainty?

2 Underline the sentence in the fifth paragraph that contains an *if* clause. Compare the meaning of this sentence with the sentence in 1. Which effect seems more likely to happen? Why?

3 Look at lines 36–41. Compare the sentence containing the *when* clause with the one containing the *if* clause that follows it. Which sentence contains an effect that is more likely to happen? Which words tell you?

D Academic Writing The writer describes one effect in each body paragraph. Underline each effect. How did the writer order them?

a chronologically   b most familiar to least
c sequence of events   d importance

CORPORATE SOCIAL RESPONSIBILITY:
The Wave of the Future

Most managers would be in agreement that the main goal of a modern company is to make a profit. If a company does not make money, it will go out of business. In addition, while pursuing
5 profit, companies should be ethical in their business practices. However, more and more people believe that the ethical pursuit of profit is no longer enough for modern companies. They argue that companies should also incorporate a strong sense of corporate
10 social responsibility (Murphy, 2019). This means managing a business while attempting to have a positive impact on the community. There are many reasons why companies may choose to embrace social responsibility.

15 According to proponents of corporate social responsibility, if companies make socially responsible decisions, they can improve life in the community. For example, companies can make an impact on a local community when they sponsor
20 local cultural events or science fairs for high school students. To make a broader impact, companies can give money to charitable organizations that are connected to the core beliefs of the company.

[1] **ally:** a person, country, or organization that provides help and support

An example of this is People Water, which helps
25 develop and support clean water programs around the world. Companies can also try to improve public policy. For instance, they may stop doing business with companies that use child labor, even if that means higher manufacturing
30 costs and lower profits.

Corporate social responsibility can also benefit the environment. For example, companies can implement green policies, such as restricting printing to important documents, buying locally
35 grown products, or conducting an electronics recycling fair. When companies conduct their business with an awareness of the environment, they set an example for the community. If these policies are part of the culture of the company,
40 employees are likely to follow them outside the workplace.

Finally, if a company makes social responsibility part of its corporate mission, it can potentially have a better public image. A socially responsible
45 company will be seen as an ally[1] of the community. This positive public image may set the company apart from its competitors. It will also attract investors, which will improve the company's finances. Companies like Patagonia, Inc. (2019) are
50 very aware of this benefit. They hire executives to focus on corporate social responsibility throughout the business.

Many companies see the value of corporate social responsibility for the community as well as
55 for their own organization. However, corporate social responsibility could play a role in every company. Supporters say that it is not just that a company makes money, but how it makes money. They argue that if more companies embraced
60 corporate social responsibility, there would be more instances of positive social change in the world.

2 Present and Future Real Conditionals

Grammar Presentation

Present and future real conditionals describe possible situations or conditions in the present and future and their likely results. They are often used to express cause and effect relationships in academic writing.

Companies **improve** life in the community **if** they **are** socially responsible.

If companies **follow** green policies, they **will set** a good example for their employees.

2.1 Present Real Conditionals

The present real conditional is formed as follows:
If clause (present), + main clause (present)

IF CLAUSE (PRESENT)
If companies **donate** to charity programs,

MAIN CLAUSE (PRESENT)
they **set** good examples for other companies.

The *if* clause can come first or last in the sentence. When the *if* clause comes first, use a comma to separate the clauses. If it comes last, do not use a comma.

Note: You can use *then* to start the main clause. The meaning does not change.

Companies **set** a good example for other companies **if** they **donate** to charity programs.

If companies donate to charity programs, **then** they set a good example for other companies.

2.2 Using Present Real Conditionals

A You can use present real conditionals to describe general truths, habits, routines, and scientific facts.

If companies **recycle,** employees generally **recycle**, too.

B In real conditional sentences, the *if* clause describes what action or event is necessary (the condition) for the action or event in the main clause to happen (the result).

IF CLAUSE: CONDITION
If companies **contribute** to charity,

MAIN CLAUSE: RESULT
many programs **benefit**.

C You can use *when* or *whenever* to replace *if* when something is a general fact or a routine.

Companies help the community **if/when/whenever** they are socially responsible.

2.3 Future Real Conditionals

A The future real conditional is formed as follows:

If clause (present) + main clause (*be going to*/*modal* + base form of verb)

The *if* clause can come first or last. Use a comma only when the *if* clause comes first.

IF CLAUSE (PRESENT)
*If we **get** a tax refund this year,*

MAIN CLAUSE (*BE GOING TO* + BASE FORM)
*(then) we **are going to buy** an electric car.*

MAIN CLAUSE (MODAL + BASE FORM)
*We **will**/**might buy** a hybrid car*

IF CLAUSE (PRESENT)
*if we **get** a tax refund this year.*

B The *if* clause states a possible future situation or condition, and the main clause states the likely result.

CONDITION   RESULT
***If I get a raise**, we will be able to buy a new car.*

2.4 Using Future Real Conditionals

A You can use future real conditionals to offer predictions. They describe possible future situations and their likely result.

***If** a company **does not make** a profit, it **will go** bankrupt.*

B You can use different modals in the main clause. The modal indicates how likely the result is.

will = It is certain.

can/*could* = It is possible.

should = It is a strong possibility.

may/*might* = It is not certain.

*If a company has a good public image, it **will** attract investors.*

*If a company addresses social responsibility, it **can** result in a better public image.*

*If the company installs solar panels at its factories, this **should** cut energy costs in half within two years.*

*Employees **might** consider ways to make their companies greener if they receive rewards for their ideas.*

Exercise 2.1 Present Real Conditionals

A Each pair of sentences below describes a way (condition) for companies to be socially responsible and the effect that the condition can have. Write *C* next to each condition and *E* next to each effect.

1. _____C_____ Car companies produce electric cars.

   _____E_____ The companies help decrease the amount of pollution in the atmosphere.

2. __________ Workers are happier and more productive.

   __________ Companies offer generous salaries.

3. __________ The government gives tax breaks to companies that donate to organizations.

   __________ Company donations to schools increase.

4. __________ Employees feel good about themselves, and the community benefits.

   __________ Companies encourage their employees to volunteer.

5. __________ The countries that allow child labor feel more pressure to change their laws.

   __________ Companies refuse to do business in countries that allow child labor.

6. __________ The companies help the environment and save money.

   __________ Companies use environmentally friendly (green) technology.

B Combine the pairs of sentences in A. Write sentences using an *if* clause in the way indicated in parentheses. Remember to use commas where necessary.

1. (*if* clause first) *If car companies produce electric cars, they help decrease the amount of pollution in the atmosphere.*

2. (main clause first) ____

3. (*if* clause first) ____

4. (main clause first) ____

5. (*if* clause first) ____

6. (main clause first) ____

C Pair Work Take turns reading the sentences in B aloud with a partner. Replace *if* in the sentences with *when* or *whenever*. Talk with a partner. Does the meaning of each sentence change? Why or why not?

Exercise 2.2 Future Real Conditionals

A Johnny's Chicken Restaurant has poor sales. Below are some suggested actions and results to improve sales. Match the actions and results.

Suggested Actions

_____*f*_____ **1** Offer inexpensive lunch specials.

__________ **2** Donate the profit of a sandwich to a nonprofit organization.

__________ **3** Have some vegetarian choices.

__________ **4** Create a website.

__________ **5** Install energy-efficient ovens.

__________ **6** Use bikes – not cars – to deliver food.

__________ **7** Buy local produce.

Results

a Save money on gas.

b Attract customers who don't eat meat.

c Lower its electricity bills.

d Show people that it supports local farmers.

e Improve its public image.

f See an increase in its lunch business.

g Get more online orders.

B Combine the actions and results in A and write suggestions for improving the restaurant. Use future real conditionals and modals that best express the meanings of the words in parentheses.

1 (strong possibility) *If the company offers inexpensive lunch specials, it should see an increase in its lunch business.*

2 (possible) __________

3 (strong possibility) __________

4 (not certain) __________

5 (possible) __________

6 (certain) __________

7 (certain) __________

C Pair Work Work with a partner. Think of a company you know that is not doing well. On a separate sheet of paper, list three reasons why the company is having problems. Next to each reason, write a suggestion to the manager to fix the problem. Use a future real conditional and the appropriate modal to show how confident you are that your suggestion would work. Next, trade papers with another pair. Read their reasons and suggestions. Do you agree that the suggestions would work? Explain your opinions.

For the problem of rude waiters, your suggestion is If you train your waiters to be kind and helpful, your business will improve. *We agree that training is helpful, but we think* could *is more accurate because we don't think training is enough to change people's behavior. We believe that employees will change if they also feel respected by management.*

3 Present and Future Unreal Conditionals

Grammar Presentation

Present and future unreal conditional sentences describe situations that are not true. They describe imaginary situations, and then give the results of those situations as if they were true. In cause and effect writing, unreal conditional sentences are used to propose changes and predict the results of those changes.

If employees became involved in the community, they would feel good about themselves.

If the restaurant donated money to a community organization, its public image would improve.

3.1 Present and Future Unreal Conditionals

A The unreal conditional is formed as follows:

If clause (past) + main clause (modal + base form of the verb). The modal *would* is the most commonly used.

The *if* clause can come first or last. Use a comma only when the clause comes first.

IF CLAUSE (PAST)
*If we **were** socially responsible,*

MAIN CLAUSE (MODAL + BASE FORM)
*we **would** attract more customers.*

*Charitable programs **would** help more people if more companies **contributed** to their programs.*

B Use *were*, not *was*, for singular subjects, including *I*, in formal writing. *Was* is more common in speaking and informal writing.

FORMAL: *If I **were** socially responsible, I would recycle.*

MORE COMMON: *If I **was** socially responsible, I would recycle.*

C The modals *would*, *might*, and *could* are used in the main clause:
Would expresses a more certain or desired effect or result. It is often used in unreal conditionals.
Might and *could* express less certain results.
Could not expresses impossibility.

*Communities **would** benefit if more companies donated time and money to local charities.*

*If your company advertised more, you **might** get more business.*

*If the organization did not receive donations, it **could not** exist.*

3.2 Using Present and Future Unreal Conditionals

A In unreal conditional sentences, use the *if clause* to describe a situation that is not real or true. However, the situation may be possible in the present or future. The main clause describes the result of the situation.

IF CLAUSE: CONDITION
*If the company **used** more resources on social issues,*

MAIN CLAUSE: RESULT
*it **would** attract more investors.*

*(It does **not** currently use many resources on social issues, but it might in the future.)*

B Present unreal conditionals are often used in cause and effect writing to propose changes and predict the results of those changes.

*Less energy **would** be consumed in the world **if** more companies **used** green technology.*

(Not enough companies use green technology in the present. The situation is not real or true at the present time.)

Grammar Application

Exercise 3.1 Present and Future Unreal Conditionals

A Read the article with tips on how individuals can be more socially responsible. Underline four more sentences containing present unreal conditional clauses.

It always feels good to help other people and know that you are making a positive difference in someone's life. Here are a few tips to get you started. First, decide who you want to help. If you want to help your community, visit a local school and ask if they need help. The school would probably appreciate your help. If there were more volunteers
5 in classrooms, teachers could spend more time with students who need special help. If there's a park or other public place near you that is full of trash, get a group of friends together and volunteer to clean it up. Your actions would have a huge impact. If these places were cleaned up, more people would visit them. As a result of all these visitors, local shops would get more business and hire more staff.
10 If you want to help people outside of your community or country, find an organization that sends money, supplies, and clothes to troubled areas. Your contributions are crucial. If these organizations didn't get donations and help, they couldn't be as effective as they are.
You could also spend your time or money helping an organization that works for
15 a special cause like cancer or heart disease. If you spent time volunteering for one of these organizations, you might learn more about the organizations and find ways to help them receive more donations. These donations could be used to fund research and lead to breakthroughs or cures. If you made a donation today, you would know that your money is going toward an important cause.

B Pair Work Explain your choices to a partner. Do you agree or disagree?

A You will listen to a radio interview about ways to improve your community. First, read the questions. Then listen and take notes on the answers. Finally, write answers to the questions using unreal conditional sentences and the modals *would*, *might*, or *could*, depending on the certainty of the speaker's comments.

1 Why is it important for more people to safely recycle their old electronics?

If more people safely recycled their old electronics, it would reduce toxins in the environment.

2 Why is it important for more people to donate their old clothes to community organizations?

3 Why should more people volunteer at a school?

4 Why should teenagers volunteer?

5 Why should more people donate money to community organizations?

B Group Work With your group, decide how the community can encourage people to become involved in solving issues that affect the quality of living. How could the community get more young and old people involved? What would motivate residents to get involved? Explain why you think people – both young and old – are not involved. Then think of five suggestions explaining how you might motivate them and how you would reward them. Present your ideas to another group or the class.

We think that teenagers are very busy with school, so they don't have time. But they also want to socialize and feel accepted. Teenagers would become more involved if the volunteering was combined with a social event. The city could . . .

4 Common Phrases with *Unless* and *If* 

Vocabulary Presentation

Unless, if . . . not, only if, and *even if* can also introduce conditions.	**Unless** *cities require solar panels for new construction, builders may continue to use older forms of energy delivery.* *People will recycle* **only if** *it is required by law.* **Even if** *companies do a lot for the community, they still need to make a profit.*

4.1 Negative Conditions: *Unless, If . . . not*

Unless can be used to describe a possible negative condition in the present or future. It suggests that failing to meet the condition will lead to an undesirable or unpleasant result.

NEGATIVE CONDITION
Unless *the organization gets more donations,*

UNDESIRABLE RESULT
it will have to cut some programs.

Unless *someone speaks up, the city will not fix the problems.* (= **If no one** *speaks up, the city will not fix the problems.*)

If with a negative subject (*no one*) or *if . . . not* has the same meaning as *unless*.

Unless *more employees volunteer for the event, it will be canceled.* (= **If** *more employees* **don't** *volunteer for the event, it will be canceled.*)

4.2 Exclusive Condition: *Only if*

Only if is used to show that the result / effect will happen when a specific condition becomes true. No other condition will have this result.

When a sentence begins with *only if*, do not use a comma. The modal in the independent clause comes before the subject.

Consumers will change their habits **only if** *prices increase dramatically.*

ONLY IF + CONDITION   MODAL + SUBJECT
Only if *prices increase dramatically* **will consumers** *change their habits.*

4.3 Emphatic Condition: *Even if*

Even if emphasizes that the condition does not matter. The condition may occur or be fulfilled, but the result will be the same.

EVEN IF + CONDITION
Even if *many people start driving electric cars,*

UNCHANGED RESULT
the country's energy needs will not decrease. (Despite the fulfillment of the condition, the expected change will not occur.)

In contrast, there is an expectation that the change will occur with *if* clauses.

IF + CONDITION   EXPECTED RESULT
If *many people start driving electric cars, the country's energy needs will be lower.* (We would expect this change.)

Vocabulary Application

Exercise 4.1 *Unless, Only If, Even If*

A Complete the sentences about the rules for refunds and exchanges for employees of a retail company that values social responsibility. Use *unless*, *only if*, and *even if*.

1 ___*Even if*___ the product is broken, offer to exchange the item for another one.

2 The customer can exchange the product ___________________ he or she has bought the item within the last 60 days. If it is more than 60 days, get a manager's approval before you make the exchange.

3 Offer an exchange first ___________________ the customer appears upset and asks for the money right away. In that case, give them the money.

4 ___________________ the customer has a receipt, can you offer an exchange. Do not offer one otherwise.

5 Do not offer the customer a store credit ___________________ the product is in good condition because we need to be able to resell it.

6 Give a cash refund ___________________ the customer refuses an exchange and a store credit. In general, try to avoid giving full cash refunds.

7 You cannot give a full cash refund ___________________ you have approval from a manager. His or her approval is required.

8 ___________________ the customer becomes upset, stay calm and patiently explain that you are doing everything you can to help him or her.

B Pair Work Rewrite the sentences with *unless* using *if . . . not*. You will need to change some words.

Exercise 4.2 More *Unless, Only If, Even If*

Complete the sentences about social responsibility in your city with a condition or a result. Use your own ideas and *unless*, *even if*, and *only if* where necessary.

1 Unless the city provides free recycling pick-up, ___________________________ .

2 Even if people recycle, ___________________________ .

3 If the city doesn't clean up the parks, ___________________________ .

4 Only if the city adds more buses and subway trains, ___________________________ .

5 ___________________________ will people volunteer in the community.

6 ___________________________ , there will continue to be crime downtown.

7 ___________________________ , children won't have a safe place to play.

8 ___________________________ , people will continue to throw litter on the streets.

5 Avoid Common Mistakes ⚠ 

1 **Remember that the subject and verb in an *if* clause must agree.**

buys
The restaurant will have more customers if it ~~buy~~ local produce.

2 **Remember that the base form of the verb follows a modal.**

make
If a company improves its image, it can ~~makes~~ a higher profit.

3 **Remember to use the correct form of the modal in real and unreal conditional sentences.**

will
Real: *If companies use recycled paper, they ~~would~~ save money.*

would
Unreal: *Telecommuting ~~will~~ work if employees had laptops.*

4 **Do not confuse *otherwise* with *unless*.**

unless
Our dependence on oil will not decrease ~~otherwise~~ we start making more electric cars.

Editing Task

Find and correct seven more mistakes in a body paragraph from an essay about how companies can make changes to create a better world.

Making a Better World

create
    If a company allows telecommuting, it can ~~creates~~ a better working lifestyle for its employees and a better world. If a business have a telecommuting program, it not only improves the environment, it also improves the quality of life for its employees. Take, for example, an employee who usually drives to the office. If he or

5 she can works from home a few days a week, there is one less car on the road. This reduces the levels of carbon dioxide in the air. If there is less carbon dioxide, there would be less pollution in the future. Telecommuting also improves the communities that employees live in. Often employees are too busy to get involved in their communities. If employees spent fewer hours at the office, they will spend more time in their communities. Employees can gets involved in local programs if they can

10 structure their own working days. For example, many telecommuters cannot volunteer in local schools or other neighborhood activities otherwise they have some free time during the week. If more companies offered telecommuting, both the environment and our communities will benefit.

6 Academic Writing

In this section, you will write an introduction and three body paragraphs for a cause and effect essay. Before you start writing, you will learn about different ways to order your ideas in your writing so that your ideas can be communicated as effectively as possible.

About Paragraph Order

In academic writing, a good introductory paragraph previews the points that will be covered in the body paragraphs of the essay. Writers must then consider the best order to present these points.

The following are some ways to order the main points in an essay.

1 **By time (chronological)** Points can be presented from earliest to latest or latest to earliest.

   Essay topic: History of recycling

   Order of points: Earliest to latest
   1   Littering problems in 1960s
   2   Garbage problems in the 1980s
   3   Recycling efforts in the 21st century

2 **By importance of ideas** Writers can start or end with what they consider to be the most important point.

   Essay topic: Environmental issues

   Order of points: End with the most important effect
   1   Issues of convenience (more expensive gasoline = important)
   2   Issues that could possibly harm lives (increased diseases = more important)
   3   Issues that could create widespread disaster (mass starvation, floods = most important)

3 **By familiarity** Writers can start with a point that is familiar to readers. This will help readers follow points more easily. This strategy requires determining who the readers are, and basing the ordering on, for example, the readers' location, the readers' area of expertise or interest, or their general knowledge.

   Essay topic: Green initiatives around the world (written by a Southern Californian)

   Order of points: Based on more familiar topic being first
   1   Green initiatives in the Southern California local community
   2   Green initiatives in other parts of the country
   3   Green initiatives in other parts of the world

4 **By sequence of events** Sometimes a cause leads to an effect, which then becomes a cause for something else. In this instance, writers often list causes or reasons in the order in which they occur, making a storyline that moves along as each effect or result happens.

Essay topic: How cars have become more fuel efficient

Order of points: Sequential

1   Public pressure on the government to pass stricter new laws on fuel efficiency

2   The effect of these new laws on the manufacture of cars

3   The automakers' decisions to market the newly required fuel-efficient cars

4   The public's embrace of hybrid cars in the 2000s

Exercise

For each thesis statement below, select one of the ordering patterns that the writer might use in writing the body paragraphs. Write the name of the ordering pattern on the line after the thesis statement.

familiarity	importance	sequence	time

1   Young people want to make changes to improve the future for three main reasons: to fix problems of the past, to live a healthier life now, and to provide a better environment for the next generation. ________________________

2   There are many ways a young person can make changes to create a better world: by changing personal habits, becoming involved locally, and learning more about the world.

____

3   Before joining an environmental organization, a young person should first research the organization online, meet and interview organization members, and then attend some meetings as a guest. ________________________

4   There are three main reasons why a young person might want to pursue a career in environmental protection. ________________________

Pre-writing Tasks
Choose a Topic

A Choose one of the essay topics listed below. You will write an introductory paragraph and three body paragraphs for a cause and effect essay on this topic.

- Changes that individuals can make in their lives to create a better world and the possible impact of these changes on the world

- Changes that groups of people (for example, neighborhood groups) can make to create a better world and the possible impact of these changes on the world

- A topic of your own approved by your teacher

B Brainstorm a list of ideas for your chosen topic. Then discuss your ideas with your classmates.

Organize Your Ideas

Use the ideas below to organize your ideas.

1 Select the idea you feel you can best develop.

2 Decide which ordering pattern you will use to organize the ideas. Then explain to a partner the ordering pattern you chose (by time, importance, familiarity, sequence) and why.

3 In the chart below, write a thesis statement, a hook, and three main points. The thesis statement should reflect the ordering pattern you decided to use. The main points in the body paragraphs should appear in the same order as they appear in your thesis statement.

Introductory Paragraph
Hook:
Thesis Statement:
Body Paragraph 1 Main Point:
Body Paragraph 2 Main Point:
Body Paragraph 3 Main Point:

Writing Task

Write your introductory and body paragraphs for your cause and effect essay. Follow the steps below.

1 Write your introductory paragraph, using the thesis statement and "hook" from your chart.

2 Write the body paragraphs, using your main points from your chart. Make sure the body paragraphs follow the order of the list of points in your thesis statement.

3 Include the following in your essay:

- real or unreal conditional statements in your body paragraphs;

- phrases like *unless, if . . . not, only if,* and *even if;*

- at least three of these academic words from the unit: *area, aware, benefit, community, conduct, core, corporate, cultural, culture, document, environment, ethical, finance, focus, goal, image, impact, implement, incorporate, instance, investor, labor, policy, positive, pursuit, restrict, role.*

4 After you write, review your work and make sure you avoided the mistakes in the Avoid Common Mistakes chart on page 45.

Peer Review

A Exchange your work with a partner. Answer the following questions as you read your partner's work, and then share your responses.

1 What is the thesis statement? Underline it.

2 What is the main point that the writer is making in each body paragraph? Identify the main points in each body paragraph and underline them.

3 Which order did your partner use to present his or her points: time, importance, familiarity, or sequence? Was this order a good choice for the essay topic? Why or why not?

4 Identify the real and unreal conditionals used in the essay, and any uses of *unless, if . . . not, only if,* and *even if.* Were they used properly?

5 Is anything confusing? Write a question mark (?) next to it.

6 Provide one compliment (something you found interesting or unusual).

B Use your partner's comments to help you revise your work. Use the Writer's Checklist on page A2 to review your paragraphs for organization, grammar, and vocabulary.

Cause and Effect 4: -ing Participle Phrases and Verbs That Show Cause and Effect

Alternative Energy Sources

1 Grammar in the Real World

You will read an essay that contains several cause and effect ideas about solar energy. In order to persuade the reader that solar energy is a good energy alternative, the writer uses ideas from experts.

A Before You Read **What are the advantages and disadvantages of traditional sources of energy, such as oil, natural gas, and coal? Read the essay. What does the writer believe are the advantages of solar energy?**

B Comprehension Check **Answer these questions.**

1 Why does the writer believe that it is important to switch from traditional energy sources to alternative energy sources, such as solar power?

2 What is the difference between renewable and nonrenewable resources? Give examples.

3 Does the writer believe that solar energy is a feasible alternative to traditional energy sources? Explain.

C Notice **Follow the instructions to help you notice and understand -ing participle phrases that show effects and causes.**

1 Look at the lines 39–42 and lines 46–48. They each have a sentence that talks about an effect. Circle the word in each sentence that signals that the writer is going to state an effect of using solar energy.

2 Notice the -ing form of the verbs that follow the words that you found in item 1. Underline the verb and all the words that complete each phrase. Notice how you can use *As a result* to restate each phrase as a sentence.

3 Reread the -ing phrase in the first sentence in the last paragraph. Does the phrase state a cause or an effect? How is its position different from the -ing phrases in item 1?

D Academic Writing **Notice how the writer includes the ideas of experts for support. In each case, the writer gives the source, a reporting verb, and the expert's idea. Find three examples. For each one, underline the source, circle the reporting verb, and highlight the expert's idea.**

Making the Dream a Reality: NEVER RUNNING OUT OF ENERGY

The demand for energy is always increasing. Currently, electricity is produced mainly with nonrenewable fossil fuels, such as coal, oil, and natural gas. Although this use of fossil fuels
5 can meet the world's current energy needs, it can potentially lead to negative consequences. These may include global warming, scarcity of[1] resources, and high prices. Environmental analysts warn us that the reserves of oil in the world are gradually
10 shrinking (Ritchie, 2017). Fortunately, there are other alternatives for energy sources. Many experts note that solar energy is one excellent substitute because it is feasible[2] to use and is a clean source of energy.

Solar energy is feasible for several reasons.
15 There are already solar thermal[3] power stations located in many places in the world, including in the United States, Spain, Australia, South Africa, and India. In these power stations, solar energy is converted into thermal energy, providing hot water
20 and heat for homes and offices. Representatives in the solar energy industry point out that the cost of producing solar energy is decreasing. For example, it costs around $50 to produce a mega-watt hour of electricity through solar power,
25 compared with about $100 to produce a mega-watt hour from coal (Berke, 2018). This lower cost for solar energy is encouraging because it may signal the start of a change in the way we power not only our buildings, but our vehicles, too. This
30 lower cost for solar energy will make it easier to use in more places in the future.

In addition to its feasibility, solar energy is very clean, unlike fossil fuels. It does not create pollution like coal, gas, and oil. It is true that many other materials can also produce energy, such as
35 recycled automobile tires and aluminum cans. However, these materials are nonrenewable and create pollution. Solar energy consumes far fewer nonrenewable materials, making less of an impact on the environment. For example, solar energy
40 uses long-lasting solar panels to convert energy from sunlight, thereby reducing our dependence on coal, oil, and gas.

Being such a clean energy, solar energy is a sensible alternative to fossil fuels. It reduces our
45 dependence on imported fuels and improves the quality of the air we breathe. The world needs energy sources like solar energy that can save resources, thus preserving the environment. The rise of renewable sources of energy – solar, wind,
50 and water energy in particular – shows that we are gradually finding ways to avoid running out of energy. The United Nations Environment Program (2019) stated that in 2018 more money was invested in solar power than in any other type of energy.
55 There is therefore reason to hope that renewables will eventually win the battle against nonrenewables.

---

[1]**scarcity of:** lack of

[2]**feasible:** possible to succeed

[3]**thermal:** related to or caused by heat

2 *-ing* Participle Phrases That Show Effect

Grammar Presentation

-ing participle phrases begin with the *-ing* form of a verb. They can show effects in academic writing.

Solar energy is converted into thermal energy, **providing hot water and heat for homes**.

Nuclear plants are expensive to build, **limiting their desirability**.

2.1 *-ing* Participle Phrases That Show Effect

A *-ing* participle phrases that show effect usually come after the independent clause.

INDEPENDENT CLAUSE
Solar energy is very clean,

-ING PARTICIPLE PHRASE
causing less pollution.

B A comma separates the *-ing* participle phrase from the independent clause.

The government is investing large sums of money in alternative energy projects, **creating thousands of new jobs**.

2.2 Using *-ing* Participle Phrases That Show Effect

A Use an *-ing* participle phrase to show the effect or result of the situation or action in the independent clause.

CAUSE
Some countries give tax credits for wind energy,

EFFECT / RESULT
lowering costs for consumers.

B You can use *thus* or *thereby* to start *-ing* participle phrases. These words strengthen the cause and effect relationship of the ideas.

The manufacturing of solar energy systems can create jobs, **thus** stimulating the economy.

Most solar panels have no moving parts, **thereby** lowering maintenance costs.

Grammar Application

Exercise 2.1 *-ing* Participle Phrases That Show Effect

A Listen to the lecture about wind power. Match each cause with its effect.

Causes	**Effects**

<u>_d_</u> **1** Wind power costs about the same as coal and oil.

a It provides low cost power to everyone.

b It is a steady source of power.

________ **2** The technology of wind power is improving.

c It reduces air pollution.

d This makes it an affordable source of alternative energy.

________ **3** Wind power will not involve many costs in the near future.

e It lowers the costs even further.

________ **4** Wind power produces zero carbon dioxide emissions.

________ **5** Wind energy is renewable.

B Combine the causes and effects in A and write sentences with *-ing* participle phrases that show effect. Remember to put a comma before the phrases.

1 _Wind power costs about the same as coal or oil, making it an affordable source of alternative energy._

2 ________________________________

3 ________________________________

4 ________________________________

5 ________________________________

Exercise 2.2 *-ing* Participle Phrases That Show Effect

A In each pair of sentences about alternative energy, label the sentences *C* for cause and *E* for effect.

1 __C__ Solar energy technology continues to improve.

   __E__ Solar energy provides more efficient and cost-effective choices.

2 ______ Solar energy reduces noise pollution.

   ______ Solar cells are silent when collecting energy.

3 ______ Solar energy helps keep our air clean.

   ______ Solar energy does not release any harmful gases into the atmosphere.

4 ______ Homeowners can sell excess electricity they create through solar energy.

   ______ Homeowners can produce extra income with no extra effort.

5 ______ Governments often give tax credits for solar power generation.

   ______ Tax credits lower the cost of installing a solar energy system.

6 ______ Solar energy provides a long-term source of energy.

   ______ Solar energy exists in the sunlight we enjoy every day.

7 ______ Wind power is another clean source of energy.

   ______ Wind power offers another renewable option for our future energy needs.

B Pair Work On a separate sheet of paper, combine each pair of sentences in A. Introduce the effect using *thus* or *thereby* and an *-ing* participle phrase. Compare your sentences with a partner.

1 *Solar energy technology continues to improve, thereby providing more efficient and cost-effective choices.*

3 -*ing* Participle Phrases That Show Cause

Grammar Presentation

In academic writing, *-ing* participle phrases can show causes or reasons.

Producing very little waste, *solar power creates an environmentally friendly source of energy.*

Being such a new technology, *solar energy is still in the development stage in many countries.*

3.1 -*ing* Participle Phrases That Show Cause

A *-ing* participle phrases that show cause or reason almost always come before the independent clause.

Providing an almost unlimited clean source of electricity, *solar energy will certainly grow in importance.*

B The omitted subject of the *-ing* participle phrase must be the same as the subject of the independent clause.

Being widely accessible, <u>hot rocks</u> *deep in the earth could be an unlimited source of energy.*

C Do not confuse *-ing* participle phrases and gerunds.

Gerunds can be the subject or object of a sentence.

-ING PARTICIPLE PHRASE
Investing in alternative sources of energy, the country will be ready for increases in oil prices.

GERUND PHRASE
Investing in solar energy was once considered a high risk.

3.2 Using *-ing* Participle Phrases That Show Cause

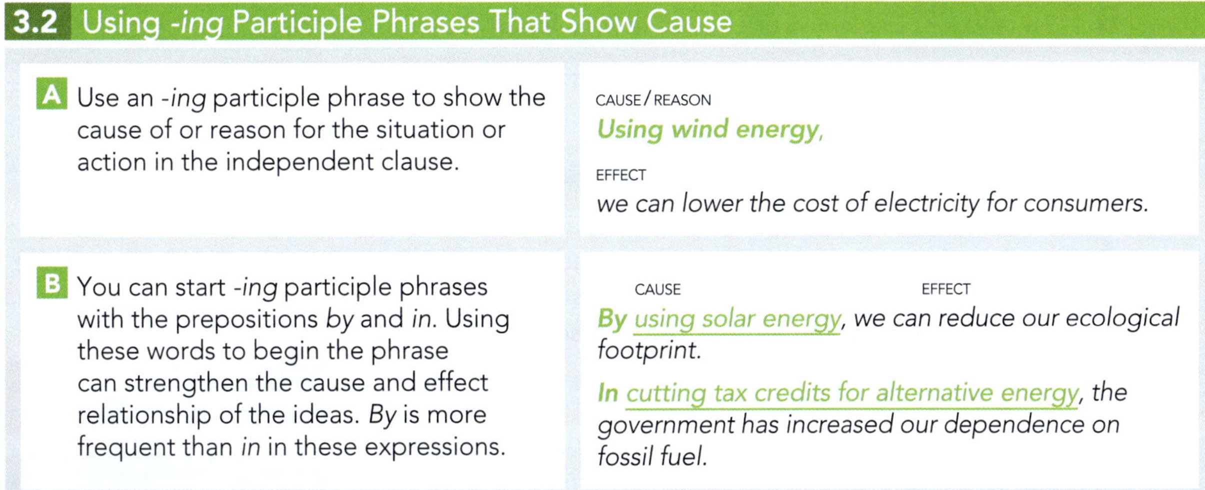

A Use an *-ing* participle phrase to show the cause of or reason for the situation or action in the independent clause.

CAUSE / REASON
Using wind energy,

EFFECT
we can lower the cost of electricity for consumers.

B You can start *-ing* participle phrases with the prepositions *by* and *in*. Using these words to begin the phrase can strengthen the cause and effect relationship of the ideas. *By* is more frequent than *in* in these expressions.

CAUSE   EFFECT
By using solar energy, *we can reduce our ecological footprint.*

In cutting tax credits for alternative energy, *the government has increased our dependence on fossil fuel.*

Grammar Application

Exercise 3.1 *-ing* Participle Phrases That Show Cause

A Read the online article about saving energy in the home. Underline each *-ing* participle phrase that expresses a cause. Circle each *-ing* participle phrase that shows an effect.

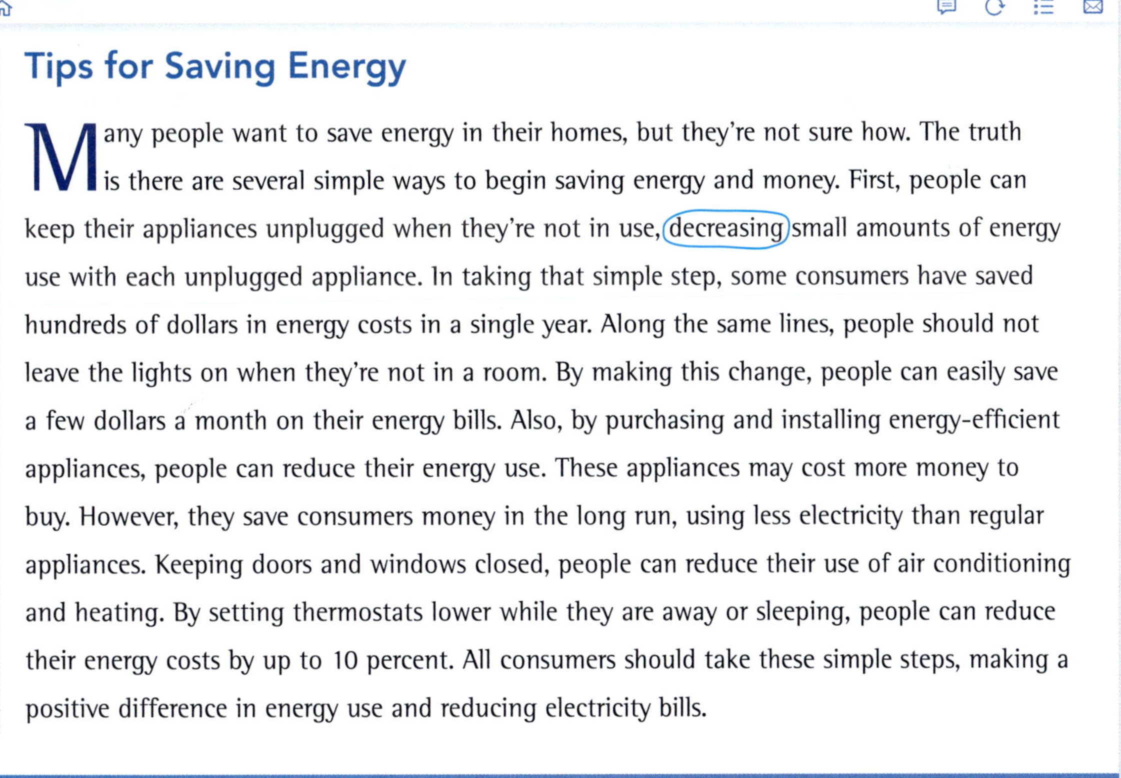

Tips for Saving Energy

Many people want to save energy in their homes, but they're not sure how. The truth is there are several simple ways to begin saving energy and money. First, people can keep their appliances unplugged when they're not in use, decreasing small amounts of energy use with each unplugged appliance. In taking that simple step, some consumers have saved hundreds of dollars in energy costs in a single year. Along the same lines, people should not leave the lights on when they're not in a room. By making this change, people can easily save a few dollars a month on their energy bills. Also, by purchasing and installing energy-efficient appliances, people can reduce their energy use. These appliances may cost more money to buy. However, they save consumers money in the long run, using less electricity than regular appliances. Keeping doors and windows closed, people can reduce their use of air conditioning and heating. By setting thermostats lower while they are away or sleeping, people can reduce their energy costs by up to 10 percent. All consumers should take these simple steps, making a positive difference in energy use and reducing electricity bills.

B Pair Work Explain your choices in A to a partner.

I circled "decreasing" because it describes the effect of unplugging appliances when they are not in use.

Exercise 3.2 *-ing* Participle Phrases That Show Cause

A Complete the sentences about ways to reduce energy consumption. Use *-ing* participle phrases and the prepositions in parentheses. Use the information from 3.1 or your own ideas. Remember to use commas after the phrases.

1 (by) *By using dimmers and timers for all the lighting,* hospitals can bring their energy costs down.

2 (in) _______________________
restaurants can reduce their use of electricity.

3 (by) _______________________
hotels would be able to reduce energy costs.

4 (by) _______________________
offices could reduce waste and energy bills.

5 (in) _______________________
airports might be able to reduce their energy costs.

6 (by) _______________________
schools could probably reduce their energy bills.

B Pair Work Discuss with a partner three things that a government can do to reduce people's energy use. Agree on three things and write sentences using *in* or *by* and *-ing* participle phrases. Share your sentences with another pair. Are any of your ideas the same?

I think that by increasing taxes on energy use, people will want to use energy more efficiently.

4 Verbs That Show Cause and Effect 

Vocabulary Presentation

The verbs *cause, lead to, produce, contribute to, result in,* and *result from* are commonly used to show cause and effect in academic writing.

*Curiously, increases in efficiency may have **led to** greater demand.*

*Higher gas prices have **contributed to** more consumer awareness of energy issues.*

4.1 Verbs That Show Cause and Effect

A *Cause* as a verb can be used in active or passive (*be + caused + by*) sentences. It is usually used to discuss negative issues (disasters, crises, etc.).

The accident **caused** a shutdown of the plant's central operations.

The slow development of alternative energy **is caused by** cheap oil.

B *Lead to* and *produce* are other ways to link cause and effect. They are more neutral than *cause* and are used to discuss positive or negative issues.

New laws **have led to** an increase in wind-generated electricity.

Overreliance on fossil fuels **could produce** an uncertain future for all of us.

C *Contribute to* is used to show one of a number of causes.

Pollution **contributes to** many health problems.

Increased use of wind power **contributes** directly **to** a cleaner environment.

D *Result in* and *result from* show a connection between cause and effect. Use *result in* to refer to the effect. Use *result from* to refer to the cause.

CAUSE   EFFECT
Strict standards for cars **will result in** a reduction in energy use.

EFFECT   CAUSE
A reduction in energy use **will result from** strict standards for cars.

Vocabulary Application

Exercise 4.1 Common Verbs That Show Cause and Effect

Rewrite the sentences about energy sources with the verb phrases in parentheses.

1 The sharp increase in oil prices in the 1970s created a surge in state-funded energy research and development. (*result in*)

The sharp increase in oil prices in the 1970s resulted in a surge in state-funded energy research and development.

2 Growing concerns about environmental issues were a factor in the government's decision in the 1970s to promote alternative energy sources. (*contribute to*)

3 Increase in oil supplies and falling prices in the 1980s were a result of a reduction in U.S. rules requiring more fuel-efficient cars. (*result from*)

4 An increase in fossil fuel usage and nuclear plants was a result of a lack of consistent solar and wind energy supplies. (*was caused by*)

5 In the future, hydrogen-based energy sources could give us pollution-free cities. (*lead to*)

____

6 Continued overreliance on oil could create political conflicts in the future. (*cause*)

____

A Read the sentences about international energy issues. Circle the correct verbs to complete the sentences.

1 The Japanese nuclear power plant accident in 2010 **resulted in** / **was caused by** widespread protests against nuclear plants.

2 Japan's position as the world's leading manufacturer of household solar technology **was a result of** / **produced** the Japanese government's financial assistance for solar roof panels in 1994.

3 High energy needs and low energy production **were caused by** / **contributed to** Japan's interest in renewable energy sources.

4 In Denmark, a high tax on electricity **produced** / **resulted from** an incentive for consumers to use less energy.

5 Denmark's interest in reducing dependence on foreign fossil fuels **resulted from** / **led to** the country's commitment to using natural sources of energy.

6 In Italy, a lack of natural resources **resulted in** / **resulted from** a need to import foreign electricity.

7 A desire to reduce use of foreign electricity **has been caused by** / **has contributed to** Italy's current focus on energy efficiency.

B Pair Work Discuss with a partner events that occurred in other countries as a result of energy issues. Use the verbs in A to explain the causes and effects.

In Ecuador in 2009 and 2010, there was an energy crisis. Severe droughts resulted in very low water levels at hydroelectric plants. This led to many blackouts.

5 Avoid Common Mistakes ⚠ 

1   **Remember to use *result in*, not *result of* for verbs that are followed by an effect.**

The increased demand for oil has resulted ~~of~~ *in* higher prices for gas.

2   **Remember to use *result from*, not *result by* for verbs that are followed by a cause.**

A decrease in carbon dioxide emissions will result ~~by~~ *from* an increase in electric cars.

3   **Remember to use *contribute to*, not *contribute for*.**

The use of solar energy will contribute ~~for~~ *to* a healthier environment.

4   **Remember that the subject and the verb must agree when using *contribute to*.**

This factor ~~contribute~~ *contributes* to climate change.

Editing Task

Find and correct six more mistakes in these paragraphs about alternative energy sources.

Rising awareness of the dangers of carbon emissions and the limits of our natural resources has contributed ~~for~~ *to* some creative ideas for alternative energy sources. While most scientists think of ways to use renewable resources in the environment to make energy, others are finding ways to generate electricity from the movements of the human body. Michael McAlpine of

5   Princeton University and some of his colleagues placed a material called PZT into flexible silicone rubber sheets. The PZT-filled sheets generate an electrical current when they are bent. Bending the sheets repeatedly results of a significant amount of energy. Placing these crystals in a pair of shoes or even directly into the body could result of enough electricity to charge devices like cell phones or tablets.

10   Our body heat can help create energy, too. For example, Belgian nanotechnology engineers built thermoelectric devices that allow a person's body heat to contribute for powering medical devices such as EKG machines and brain monitors. In 2010, engineers in Paris discovered a different way to use body heat to conserve electricity. The engineers developed a system that uses geothermal technology to move heat from a metro, or subway, station to

15   heating pipes in a public-housing project above the station. Their system resulted from a 33 percent cut in carbon dioxide emissions in the housing project's heating system. Innovative approaches like these contributes to solving our ongoing need for alternative energy sources.

6 Academic Writing

In this section, you will write a cause and effect essay. Before you write, you will learn some effective ways to paraphrase.

About Paraphrasing

Much of the supporting information in an academic essay may come from various sources. When writers include information from a source but do not directly quote it, the information needs to be paraphrased and cited. *Paraphrasing* means stating the information in a different way from the original without changing its meaning. *Citing* means stating who wrote the original material and / or what publication the original material came from. By paraphrasing and citing, writers avoid plagiarizing, that is, they avoid copying someone's exact words and using them as if they were their own.

The following will help you write effective paraphrases. In each case, the writer is paraphrasing this sentence below:

"Denmark leads the world in wind energy, generating 20 percent of its energy from wind power" (Evans, 2007, para. 2).

1   **Use synonyms.** It is helpful to look at a thesaurus for synonyms, but be careful deciding which ones to use. If you are not sure what a word means, use your dictionary. A good learner dictionary will often have additional information that can help you find appropriate synonyms. Here the writer uses *producing* instead of *generating*.

   Producing *20 percent of its energy from wind power, Denmark is the world leader in wind energy (Evans, 2007, para. 2).*

2   **Change the order of the ideas in the sentences.** Here the writer mentions Denmark's energy production before mentioning it is the world leader.

   Producing 20 percent of its energy from wind power, **Denmark is the world leader in wind energy production** *(Evans, 2007, para. 2).*

3   **Break long sentences into shorter ones. Alternatively, combine sentences, changing shorter ones into longer ones.** Here the writer has created two sentences from the original sentence.

   Denmark is the world leader in wind energy. **Twenty percent of its energy comes from wind power** *(Evans, 2007, para. 2).*

4   **Change the word form of key words, and shift grammar as needed to fit the new word forms.** Here the writer uses *leader* instead of *lead* and makes the necessary changes to the grammar.

   Denmark is the world **leader** *in wind energy. Twenty percent of its energy comes from wind power (Evans, 2007, para. 2).*

5   **Switch between active and passive voice.**

   Denmark is the world leader in wind energy. Twenty percent of its energy **is produced** *from wind power (Evans, 2007, para. 2).*

6 **Combine several of the strategies (1–5 above) to create your paraphrase.**

One-fifth of the energy in Denmark is produced from wind power. This makes Denmark a world leader in wind energy production (Evans, 2007, para. 2).

7 **Always include a citation that recognizes the source of the material that you are paraphrasing.** This should go after the first mention of the author, or if the author is not mentioned, at the end of the material being paraphrased.

*One-fifth of the energy in Denmark is produced from wind power. This makes Denmark a world leader in wind energy production **(Evans, 2007, para. 2)**.*

8 **Make sure that you do not change the meaning of the original material when you paraphrase.** The following paraphrase contains two inaccuracies. According to the source information, Denmark is *the* leader in the world and produces only *one-fifth* of its energy from wind.

Denmark is one of the leading producers of wind energy in the world; almost one-half of its domestic energy is provided by wind power (Evans, 2007, para. 2).

Exercise

A Paraphrase each quotation below, using at least two of the strategies described above.

1 "Population and income growth are the two most powerful driving forces behind the demand for energy" ("BP Energy Outlook 2030," 2011, p. 9).

2 "About 42 percent of the world's energy-related CO_2 emissions come from oil" ("Our Dependence on Oil," 2010, p. 2).

3 "Even though many technical processes have become more efficient, the energy needs per person have also greatly increased" ("Energy Today and Tomorrow," 2008, para. 2).

4 "Every time solar power output doubles, the price drops by 18 percent" (cited in Sweet, 2007, para. 11).

5 " 'Car culture,' both in the cities and suburbs, causes the smog that helps make many California cities unhealthful" ("The True Costs of Petroleum: The Community Map," 2003, p. 3).

B Pair Work Work with a partner. Read each other's paraphrases and identify which of the strategies your partner used. Did you use the same ones? Then discuss ways you each could improve your paraphrases.

Pre-writing Tasks
Choose a Topic

A Choose one of the essay topics listed below. You will write an essay that discusses several causes that lead to one effect or one cause that leads to several effects.

- Things that can be done to make energy more affordable
- The causes and effects of improving energy use in the home
- A topic of your own approved by your teacher

B Pair Work Share your topic with a partner. Describe the causes and effects that are important for your topic. Provide suggestions to each other about what to include.

Organize Your Ideas

A Research your chosen topic. Find at least two direct quotations from your sources that you might include in your essay. Complete the chart below with the name of the source, the quotation, and a paraphrase of the quotation.

Source	Quotation	Paraphrase
1		
2		

B Pair Work Work with a partner. Share your quotations and your paraphrases. Tell your partner why you chose the quotations. Have your partner check your paraphrases to make sure you are not plagiarizing.

Writing Task

Write your cause and effect essay. Follow the steps below.

1 Write an introductory paragraph with a hook and a thesis statement.

2 Write body paragraphs that express your main points.

3 Order your paragraphs in the most logical way according to your main points.

> **Academic Writing Tip**
>
> **Use Quotations and References**
>
> Taking material directly from any source without using quotations and citing it correctly is considered plagiarism. For more information on ways to avoid plagiarism, see About Plagiarism, page A3.

4 Include the following in your essay:

- ways to show cause and effect that you learned in Units 1–4;
- *-ing* participle phrases and verbs such as *contribute to and result from* to link cause and effect;
- at least three academic words from this unit: *alternative, analyst, cite, consequence, convert, create, decade, despite, dramatically, energy, environment, environmental, expert, impact, negative, percent, potential, process, research, resource, substitute;*
- paraphrases and quotations from your sources. Do not forget to include the name of the author, year of publication, and page number for your sources (if available).

5 After you write your essay, review it and make sure you avoided the mistakes in the Avoid Common Mistakes chart on page 59.

Peer Review

A Exchange your essay with a partner. Answer the following questions as you read your partner's paragraph, and share your responses.

1 What is the topic? Underline the thesis statement.

2 What are the cause(s) and effect(s) the writer addresses in the essay?

3 Does the essay contain several causes leading to one effect, or one cause leading to several effects?

4 Look at the lists of causes and effects. Did the writer choose a specific order, such as familiarity or importance?

5 What paraphrases and quotations are used in the essay? Are they effective? Why or why not?

6 Identify any *-ing* participle phrases. Do they show cause or effect?

7 Is anything confusing? Write a question mark (?) next to it.

8 Provide one compliment (something you found interesting or unusual).

B Use your partner's comments to help you revise your essay. Use the Writer's Checklist on page A2 to review your essay for organization, grammar, and vocabulary.

5

Comparison and Contrast 1: Identifying Relative Clauses; Comparatives with *As . . . As;* Common Patterns That Show Contrast

Family Size and Personality

1 Grammar in the Real World

You will read an essay that discusses how a child's birth order in the family may affect his or her personality as an adult. The essay is an example of a type of comparison and contrast writing in which the ideas are organized using the block method.

A Before You Read How many siblings do you have? Do you think that some of their personality traits come from the order of their birth? Read the essay. How strong are the effects of birth order, according to the essay?

B Comprehension Check Answer the questions.

1 How are former presidents Jimmy Carter, George W. Bush, and Barack Obama connected to the main idea of the text?

2 According to the writer, why are firstborn children usually more ambitious than their siblings?

3 Which of the different birth order types – firstborn, middle born, youngest, and only child – do you think has the fewest advantages in life? Explain.

C Notice Follow the instructions below to help you notice and understand comparison and contrast sentences from the essay that use *as . . . as.*

1 Read the *as . . . as* sentence in the third paragraph. Are middle children likely to be equally, more, or less determined than firstborn children? Explain.

2 Read the *as . . . as* sentence in the fourth paragraph. Are youngest children likely to be equally, more, or less creative than middle children? Explain.

3 Read the *as . . . as* sentence in the fifth paragraph. Are only children likely to be equally, more, or less intelligent than children with siblings? Explain.

D Academic Writing Underline the sentence that gives the main idea of each body paragraph. This sentence is called the *topic sentence.*

Birth Order

and Adult Sibling Relationships

What do U.S. Presidents Jimmy Carter, George W. Bush, and Barack Obama all have in common? In addition to being elected president of the United States, these men all share the same birth order. Each one is the oldest child in his family. In fact, many very successful people in government and business have been "firstborn" children. While there is always some variation, some experts agree that birth order can have an influence on a person's personality in childhood and in adulthood.

Firstborn children often share several traits. First, in contrast to their siblings, they are more likely to be responsible, ambitious, and authoritarian. This is probably because they are born into an environment of high expectations, and they usually receive a great deal of attention. They are used to being leaders, taking responsibility for others, and sometimes taking on an almost parental role.

Middle children, on the other hand, exhibit different characteristics from firstborns. They are often not as determined as firstborns. They tend to be more passive and solitary. Having to share family attention with older and younger siblings, middle children have a tendency to be more realistic, creative, and insightful.

Youngest children are often more protected than their older siblings. As a result, they are more likely to be dependent and controlling. They are often as creative as middle children, but usually more easygoing and social.

A child with no siblings, or an "only child," also exhibits some unique characteristics. While some parents worry that an only child will have difficulties socializing and making friends, studies show that an only child is just as intelligent, accomplished, and sociable as a child with siblings. In fact, some research indicates that being an only child has some benefits. These children tend to have better vocabulary, perform better at school, and maintain closer relationships with their parents than children with siblings.

Even though it is assumed that birth order dictates some personality traits, individuals can free themselves from the roles they played when they were young, but it can be difficult. According to Vikki Stark, family therapist and author of *My Sister, My Self*, change requires letting go of familiar ways of being and patiently asserting new behaviors that express one's true self (Kochan, para. 14).

Family Size and Personality **65**

2 Identifying Relative Clauses

Grammar Presentation

A relative clause modifies a noun and follows the noun it modifies. Identifying relative clauses provide necessary information about the noun. They are used in all kinds of academic writing, but they are especially useful in comparison and contrast writing to describe characteristics of elements that are being compared.

*Children **who/that have no siblings** are often very close to their parents. People gradually behave in ways **which/that are more consistent with their preferred self-image**.*

2.1 Identifying Relative Clauses

A An identifying relative clause modifies a noun. It begins with a relative pronoun: *that, which, who, whom,* or *whose*. (It is often called a *restrictive relative clause*.)

An identifying relative clause answers the question, "Which one?" It gives necessary information about the noun or noun phrase in the main clause. Without that information, the sentence would be incomplete.

IDENTIFYING RELATIVE CLAUSE
*People **who do not have children** may not be aware of differences in birth order.*

IDENTIFYING RELATIVE CLAUSE
*Creativity is a trait **that all middle children share**.*

B *Who, that,* and *whom* refer to people. Use *whom* for object relative clauses. In informal speaking and writing, the use of *who* for *whom* is common.

PEOPLE
*Researchers **who/that study families** have different views.*

*My siblings are the people in my life **whom I** will always trust.*

C *Whose* shows possession. It is followed by an animate or inanimate noun in academic writing.

POSSESSION
*Researchers **whose work focuses on families** disagree about the importance of birth order.*

*She cited a study **whose** results supported previous research.*

Which and *that* refer to things. In academic writing, *that* is often preferred to *which* in identifying relative clauses.

THINGS
*The study examines characteristics **that/which are common in firstborn children**.*

2.1 Identifying Relative Clauses *(continued)*

D In a subject relative clause, the relative pronoun is the subject.

In an object relative clause, the relative pronoun is the object of the verb.

Note: The relative pronoun in object relative clauses can be omitted, but it is better not to do so in academic writing. The relative pronoun may not be omitted in subject relative clauses.

Psychologists <u>who</u> work with only children and their parents can help the children learn to share attention. (Who is the subject of the verb work in the relative clause.)

There are several strategies <u>that</u> parents use to help their only children. (That is the object of the verb use in the relative clause.)

The research <u>(that) they just published on sibling order</u> was inconclusive.

E A preposition can also come at the beginning of the clause, but this is only used in very formal writing.

Note: The relative pronoun may not be omitted in the formal version.

FORMAL WRITING: *An older sibling is someone <u>on whom</u> you can always rely.*

MORE COMMON: *An older sibling is someone <u>that/who</u> you can always rely <u>on</u>.*

Researchers studied the ways <u>in which</u> parents interacted with their only child.

DATA FROM THE REAL WORLD

In academic writing, 75 percent of relative clauses with *whose* modify inanimate nouns.

The report included the results of a study funded by an organization <u>whose</u> mission is to help children reach their potential.

2.2 Using Identifying Relative Clauses

A Use identifying relative clauses in comparison and contrast writing to provide characteristics or information that shows the differences between the elements you are comparing.

My friend <u>who lives in Boston</u> always remembers my birthday, but my friend <u>who lives in New Jersey</u> does not.

Some people like to play games <u>that involve competition,</u> while others like to play games <u>that encourage collaboration.</u>

B Relative clauses are similar to subordinate clauses in that they are fragments if they appear alone.

FRAGMENT: *A recent study reports that firstborns are generally smarter than siblings. <u>Who are born later.</u>*

CORRECT: *A recent study reports that firstborns are generally smarter than siblings <u>who are born later.</u>*

In academic writing, the relative pronoun **who** is more commonly used than **that** to refer to people.

In speaking, the relative pronoun **that** is more commonly used than **who** to refer to people.

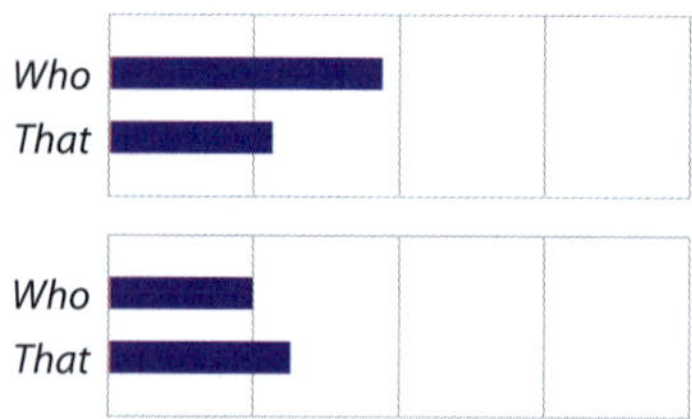

 Grammar Application

Exercise 2.1 Identifying Relative Clauses

A Read the paragraph about birth order. Complete each sentence with *that*, *who*, *whom*, or *whose*. Sometimes more than one answer is possible.

Birth order researchers have discovered some interesting information ___*that*___ (1) can help us understand our colleagues better. Do you have a difficult boss ___________ (2) authoritarian personality makes your life difficult? If so, your boss might be a firstborn child. Children ___________ (3) are born first are often more authoritarian than their younger siblings. Do you have a co-worker ___________ (4) is passive, but particularly creative and insightful? This person may be a middle child. People ___________ (5) have both older and younger siblings are often passive because their older siblings were responsible for their well-being when they were young. The creativity ___________ (6) they exhibit might be the effect of their having spent a lot of time on their own due to having to share parental attention with their older and younger siblings. People ___________ (7) you work with ___________ (8) are controlling may be youngest children. These people are also likely to be more social than co-workers ___________ (9) are middle children. Of course, these are only generalizations. There are countless factors ___________ (10) help form people's personalities, but birth order research may shed some helpful light on people's behavior in the workplace.

B Look at the relative pronouns you wrote in A. Write *S* above each relative pronoun that is the subject of the clause, *O* above each relative pronoun that is the object of the clause, and *P* above each relative pronoun that shows possession.

Exercise 2.2 More Identifying Relative Clauses

A Combine each pair of sentences that describe opinions about parental behavior using an identifying relative clause.

1 Some parents often focus too much attention on their son or daughter. These parents have only one child.

   Some parents who have only one child often focus too much attention on their son or daughter.

2 Parents put a lot of pressure on their children to do a lot of activities. These parents want their children to excel.

3 Children often feel a lot of stress. Their parents have high expectations of them.

4 Sports practice and music lessons are examples of activities. Some parents expect their children to do these activities after school.

5 Parents raise more independent adults. These parents give proper emotional support to their children.

6 Some children have behavioral problems at school. Their parents both work long hours.

B Pair Work Tell a partner whether you agree or disagree with each opinion in A. Use identifying relative clauses where possible.

A *I don't think it's true that parents who have only one child focus too much attention on that child. I was an only child, and I don't think that I received too much attention from my parents.*

B *I disagree. In my experience, parents who have an only child often want to give that child everything. The child doesn't realize what it's like to share, either.*

3 Comparatives with *As . . . As*

Grammar Presentation

Writers show similarities and differences in comparison and contrast writing by using *as . . . as.*

*Some people think that youngest children might not be **as mature as** their siblings. Sometimes younger children do not get **as much attention as** their older siblings.*

3.1 *As . . . As*

A *As . . . as* can be used in the following patterns:

(not) as + adjective/adverb + as

ADJECTIVE
*Youngest children are not as **independent***

NOUN PHRASE
*as **their older siblings.***

ADVERB
*An only child socializes as **well** as children with siblings.*

(not) as + noun phrase + as

NOUN PHRASE
*An only child has as **many close friends** as children with siblings.*

B *As . . . as* can also be used to compare quantities with count and noncount nouns:

(not) as much + noncount noun phrase + as

*Younger children sometimes don't get as **much attention** from parents as firstborn children.*

(not) as many + count noun phrase + as

*Growing up as an only child has as **many advantages** as growing up in a large family.*

3.2 Using *As . . . As*

Use *as . . . as* in the following ways:
to emphasize two equal elements:
——— *(just) as . . . as* ———

to show that two things are slightly unequal:
——— *almost/nearly/about/not quite as . . . as*
to emphasize a difference:
——— *not nearly as . . . as* ———

*Only children usually turn out **just as well as** children from large families.*

*Firstborn children are **almost as open to new experiences as** their younger siblings.*

*Genuine concern over sibling order may **not be nearly as widespread as** it seems at first glance.*

Grammar Application

Exercise 3.1 Comparatives with *As . . . As*

A Complete the sentences about personality traits and birth order using the information in the chart and *as . . . as* phrases.

	Firstborn Children	Middle Children	Youngest Children
Responsible	Very	Somewhat	Not Very
Social	Somewhat	Not Very	Very
Creative	Not Very	Very	Very
Realistic	Very	Very	Not Very
Dependent	Not Very	Not Very	Very

1 Middle children _**are not as responsible as**_ (responsible) firstborns.

2 Firstborn children ______________________
(social) youngest children.

3 Middle children ______________________
(creative) youngest children.

4 Youngest children ______________________
(realistic) middle children.

5 Middle children ______________________
(dependent) firstborn children.

6 Firstborn children ______________________
(realistic) middle children.

7 Firstborn children ______________________ (creative) youngest children.

8 Middle children ______________________ (dependent) youngest children.

B Look at the information in the chart in A about firstborn children, middle children, and youngest children again. Think about your birth order and the birth order of people you know. Does the information accurately describe your personality and their personalities? Why or why not? Give at least one example for each birth order.

I'm a middle child and my brother is a firstborn child. According to the chart, I'm not as responsible as firstborn children, but actually, I'm much more responsible than my brother. Maybe it's because I was given the responsibility of taking care of everyone while my parents worked. I think I have always felt responsible for my siblings. I agree with the idea that youngest children are social. My younger brother is really outgoing and has a lot of friends . . .

A Listen to the story of two famous sisters – Venus and Serena Williams. Complete the chart.

	Venus Williams	Serena Williams
1 Birth date	*June 17, 1980*	
2 Height	*6'1"*	
3 Year turned professional		
4 Wimbledon singles victories (individual years)		
5 U.S. Open singles victories (individual years)		

B On a separate sheet of paper, use the information from A and the cues below to write sentences with the following *as . . . as* phrases: *almost as . . . as; just as . . . as; not nearly as . . . as* and *not quite as . . . as*. Sometimes more than one answer is possible.

1 Serena / is / tall / Venus.

   Serena is not quite as tall as Venus.

2 Serena / has / played / long / Venus.

3 Serena / is / old / Venus.

4 Serena / has / experience / Venus.

5 Serena / is / important to U.S. sports / Venus.

6 Serena / has / won / Wimbledon singles / Venus.

7 Venus / is / famous / Serena.

8 Serena / has had / Wimbledon singles victories / Venus has had.

9 Venus / has had / success in business / Serena. They are both successful businesswomen.

Serena and Venus Williams

C Pair Work Tell a partner about two people you know well. Compare them using *as . . . as* structures. Next, write five sentences about them using *as . . . as*. Use adjectives, adverbs, and noun phrases as well as phrases such as *almost, not nearly*, and *not quite* in your sentences where possible.

Younsil does not have as many children as Victoria.
Younsil is not quite as shy as Victoria.

4 Common Patterns That Show Contrast 

Vocabulary Presentation

Useful words and phrases that show contrast in academic writing include *difference(s)*, *differ*, *in contrast*, and *unlike*. These words are important in comparison and contrast writing.

One **major difference** in some cultures is the role of adult children.

In contrast to the past, more U.S. children now live with their parents into their early adulthood.

4.1 Difference(s), Differ, In Contrast, Unlike

A A common pattern with the noun *difference* is:

NOUN PHRASE

The difference between __________
NOUN PHRASE
and __________ *is . . .*

One **significant difference between** youngest children **and** their older siblings **is** that youngest children receive a lot of attention.

B A common pattern with the verb *differ* is:

NOUN PHRASE   NOUN PHRASE
__________ *differ(s) from* __________ *in that . . .*

The results of current research **differ from** earlier results **in that** they show a definite relationship between birth order and personality.

C Common expressions and patterns used with the phrase *in contrast* are:

NOUN PHRASE   INDEPENDENT CLAUSE
In contrast to __________ , __________ .

INDEPENDENT CLAUSE
In contrast, __________ .

In contrast to traditional American families, the Chinese have had several generations of one-child families.

Many children without siblings receive a lot of attention. **In contrast**, children with siblings often share their parents' attention.

D A common pattern with the adjective *unlike* is:

NOUN PHRASE   INDEPENDENT CLAUSE
Unlike __________ , __________ .

Unlike firstborn children, youngest children are generally very creative.

DATA FROM THE REAL WORLD

Adjectives and quantifiers that most frequently occur with *difference* are:
significant, major, important, many, large, small, some, minor, cultural, regional, individual.

There are many **cultural differences** in how parents treat their children.

One **major difference** between the siblings is that the older ones tend to be more confident.

Vocabulary Application

A Complete the following sentences about children in the United States using the words and phrases in the box.

differ from	~~major difference between~~	unlike
in contrast	significantly different from	

1 One _**major difference between**_ children in the United States in 1900 and now is that children in the past didn't get a lot of individual attention from their parents, while children today get a lot of individual attention.

2 Another way that today's children are

____

children in the past is that in the past, children often worked to help their families, but children now often work for their own extra spending money.

3 Today's children also _______________________ children in 1900 in that they are required to attend school.

4 Children in the past often had large families with several siblings. _______________________________ , many children today have one or two siblings or are only children.

5 In 1900, children were very independent. ____ them, children today depend on their parents a lot.

B Pair Work With a partner, draw a chart like the one below. Write five contrasting pieces of information about children in the 1900s and now in a culture that you are familiar with. Then present your information to the class, using vocabulary from A.

Children in the 1900s	Children Now

One major difference between young children in my native country today and in the 1900s is that in the 1900s, they used to work in factories. Today that's illegal.

5 Avoid Common Mistakes ⚠ 

1   **Do not use *who* with inanimate nouns.**

      that

A study ~~who~~ showed the benefits of being an only child was published last year.

2   **Do not omit the relative pronoun in subject relative clauses.**

      who

Children ˄ have older siblings tend to be somewhat dependent.

3   **Remember that the subject and the verb must agree in relative clauses.**

      have

Children who ~~has~~ siblings often become secure and confident adults.

4   **Use *the same as*, not *the same than*.**

      as

Middle children often have the same level of creativity ~~than~~ youngest children.

Editing Task

Find and correct eight more mistakes in this body paragraph from an essay comparing trends in families in the past and today.

Families Past and Present

     A major way that families have changed is the number of families *that* ˄ have only one child. The number of families had only one child was low in the United States in the 1950s and 1960s. However, one-child families began increasing in the 1970s and are very common today. This is especially true in households who have only one parent.

5   One reason families are smaller is the cost of living. It is not the same than it was 40 years ago. For example, it costs about 10 times more to send a child to college than it did 40 years ago. As a result, many parents choose to have only one child because they do not have enough money for more children.

10   In addition, attitudes about only children are also not the same than attitudes about them in the past. In the 1950s and 1960s, people avoided having only one child. At that time, many people thought that children did not have siblings had many disadvantages. For example, people thought that they did not learn good social skills. However, recent studies who focus on only children show a different picture.

15   These studies show that only children tend to have the same social skills than children who has siblings.

6 Academic Writing

In this section, you will write an outline and one body paragraph for a comparison and contrast essay using the block method. Before you start writing, you will learn how to write effective topic sentences.

About Topic Sentences

Topic sentences introduce the main idea of a body paragraph. In academic essays, they often appear at the beginning of body paragraphs. Although not all body paragraphs have topic sentences, it will help you to organize your writing if you always include one.

The following guidelines will help you write effective topic sentences:

1   An effective topic sentence should contain a claim or an opinion that needs to be supported with evidence. It should not be a fact that is widely accepted as true. Notice the difference in the following sentences:

- Some families are small. (a fact)

- Small families are better than large families. (a claim that needs to be supported with evidence)

2   The content of the topic sentences should relate back to the thesis statement of the essay.

- Siblings have different personality traits because of birth order. (thesis statement)

- Firstborn children are generally leaders. (topic sentence)

3   The topic sentence is usually a general statement. It rarely contains detailed information. The details will come in the rest of the paragraph in sentences that convince the reader that the claim in the topic sentence is valid or true.

- Middle children can be more solitary. (general statement)

- Middle children do not always get a lot of attention. (detail to support the topic sentence)

4   Include words and phrases that connect one body paragraph to another.

- *Unlike* middle children, those born last are often more easygoing.

- *In addition to* being more easygoing, the youngest are also . . .

- *Another* common trait of the youngest child is . . .

Exercise

A Pair Work With a partner, critique the following topic sentences that support the thesis statement below. Discuss which are strong and which are weak according to the guidelines above.

Thesis statement: *Being brought up in a large family has several advantages and some disadvantages.*

1 One major disadvantage of growing up in a large family is that there is not much privacy.

2 When I was growing up, on the weekends my siblings and I would all go to the park and play soccer together.

3 While there are certainly several disadvantages to being part of a very large family, there are many advantages, too.

4 My next-door neighbor has six siblings.

5 In a study of children growing up in large families, it was found that in 86 percent of the cases, the eldest child had the highest I.Q.

B Read the following thesis statement, and then write topic sentences for the body paragraphs. Use the topic given in parentheses.

Thesis statement: *Being an only child has several benefits: developing independence, encouraging creativity, and creating friendships outside the family.*

1 Body paragraph 1 (independence): *Being an only child provides many opportunities to become independent.*

2 Body paragraph 2 (creativity): ___________________________

3 Body paragraph 3 (friendships): ___________________________

Pre-writing Tasks
Choose a Topic

A Choose one of the essay topics listed below. You will write one body paragraph for a comparison and contrast essay on this topic. This essay will follow the block method.

- The characteristics of large and small families

- Traditions in two different families

- A topic approved by your teacher

B Pair Work Share your topic with a partner. Describe the similarities and differences you will write about.

Organize Your Ideas

A For this assignment, you will use the block method of comparison and contrast for organizing your ideas.

Look at the block method outline for the essay on birth order below. Use the blank outline that follows to create an outline for your topic.

Title of Essay: Birth Order

Paragraph 1. Introductory paragraph. Thesis Statement: Experts agree that birth order tends to dictate some basic personality traits in children and adults.

Paragraph 2. Topic Sentence: Firstborn children often share several common traits.
- Traits: responsible, ambitious, authoritarian

Paragraph 3. Topic Sentence: Middle children exhibit unique characteristics.
- Traits: passive, solitary, realistic, creative, insightful

Paragraph 4. Topic Sentence: Youngest children have typical characteristics as well.
- Traits: dependent, controlling, creative, easygoing, social

Title of Essay: _______________________________

Paragraph 1. Introductory paragraph. Thesis Statement: _______________________________

Paragraph 2. Topic Sentence: _______________________________

- **Details:** _______________________________

Paragraph 3. Topic Sentence: _______________________________

- **Details:** _______________________________

Paragraph 4. Topic Sentence: _______________________________

- **Details:** _______________________________

B Pair Work Share your outline with a partner and discuss your ideas.

Writing Task

Write one of the body paragraphs from your outline. Follow the steps below.

1 Make sure that you have a clear topic sentence that follows the guidelines in About Topic Sentences on page 76.

2 Include the following in your paragraph:

■ identifying relative clauses;

■ *as . . . as*;

■ common patterns that show contrast;

■ at least three of these academic words from the essay in this unit: *adulthood, assumed, author, benefit, creative, environment, exhibit, expert, indicate, individual, insightful, intelligent, maintain, passive, research, role, unique.*

3 After you write your paragraph, review it and make sure that you avoided the mistakes in the Avoid Common Mistakes chart on page 75.

> **Academic Writing Tip**
>
> **Improving Your Internet Searches**
>
> When you do an Internet search, use quotation marks around important ideas. For example, "large families" will eliminate results with only "large" or "family" alone.

Peer Review

A Exchange your outline and paragraph with a partner. Answer the following questions as you read your partner's outline and work, and share your responses.

1 Is the outline organized using the block method?

2 Does the topic sentence relate to the thesis statement?

3 Are any identifying relative clauses, *as . . . as*, or common patterns that show contrast used in the paragraph?

4 Is anything confusing? Write a question mark (?) next to it.

5 Provide one compliment (something you found interesting or unusual).

B Use your partner's comments to help you revise your paragraph. Use the Writer's Checklist on page A2 to review your paragraph for organization, grammar, and vocabulary.

Comparison and Contrast 2: Complex Noun Phrases; Parallel Structure; Common Quantifiers

Men, Women, and Equality

1 Grammar in the Real World

You will read an essay about how men and women often treated differently in society. The essay is an example of one type of comparison and contrast writing, in which ideas are organized using the point-by-point method.

A Before You Read **Are men and women treated differently in today's society? Read the essay. What does the writer think?**

B Comprehension Check **Answer the questions.**

1 According to the writer, what is gender inequality? Where is it found?
2 How does the writer say that women and men are treated differently in the workplace?
3 Give two examples of how boys and girls are treated differently.

C Notice **Follow the instructions below to find ways that the author uses parallel structure to contrast the differences in genders.**

1 Find the sentence on lines 23–25 that states how men are expected to behave in the workplace. Then look on lines 27–30 for the sentence that describes how women are expected to behave. How many adjectives describe men's expected behavior? How many adjectives describe women's behavior? What other similarities do the two sentences have?

2 Find the sentence on lines 42–45 in which the author compares the types of toys that boys and girls receive as presents. How many toys are mentioned for boys and how many for girls?

3 Find the sentence in the third paragraph that contrasts how boys and girls are expected to behave. How many adjectives describe boys' expected behavior? How many adjectives describe girls'? What other similarities do the two clauses in the sentence have?

D Academic Writing **In a body paragraph, each main idea is developed by providing supporting information. Read the second paragraph again. Underline the topic sentence, and write a number in the margin for each supporting detail that follows it.**

Gender Inequality

Although progress has been made in recent decades, it would be wrong to think that men and women today are treated equally in the United States or in other industrialized nations.

5 Historically, men in the United States have always had more financial, legal, and political power and more job opportunities than women. However, since the 1960s, there has been a progressive increase in the number of women working
10 outside the home, running their own businesses, and participating in political life. Nevertheless, despite women's increasing participation, gender inequality can still be found in the workplace as well as in cultural and social aspects of life.

15 Women and men are not always treated equally at work. The clearest sign of inequality in the workplace is at the top levels of management. For example, the vast majority of major corporations have male CEOs (Chief Executive Officers),
20 and most of the top positions are filled by men (Catalyst, 2019). Another sign of gender inequality is the different expectations employers have of men and women in leadership positions. Men are usually expected to be assertive, confident,
25 and decisive. When men take a dominant role, they are often rewarded by their employers. Assertive women, on the other hand, are often not well received in the workplace because they are expected to be flexible, cooperative, and
30 deferential.[1] There are also significant differences in salary. According to the Institute for Women's Policy Research, women still make less than men even when they do the exact same job. For example, in 2017, full-time female employees made 80.5 cents compared to every dollar made
35 by male employees or, in other words, a wage difference of 20 percent (IWPR, 2019, p. 1).

Gender differences are found in our cultural and social lives as well. Boys and girls are taught different gender roles and social expectations
40 from birth. For example, in the United States many baby boys still receive blue clothes and blankets, while many girls receive pink ones. Boys are often given cars, trucks, and toy soldiers as presents, while girls often receive dolls, dollhouses, and
45 toy ovens. In terms of behavior, in many cultures people tend to expect boys to be aggressive and dominant, whereas they generally expect girls to be emotional and subordinate.[2] As children grow up and become adults, these behavior patterns
50 are usually reinforced through social interactions.

Gender inequality has existed in the United States and other industrialized countries for many years, and it will not disappear overnight. Progress has been made recently regarding the
55 opportunities for women. However, both men and women should continue to work for equality to create a fairer environment for everyone.

---

[1]**deferential:** polite and showing respect
[2]**subordinate:** lower in position; following orders

2 Complex Noun Phrases

Grammar Presentation

Noun phrases include a noun and modifiers. Some modifiers, like adjectives, usually come before the noun, but there are other modifiers that can come after the noun. Complex noun phrases can have modifiers both before and after the noun. Complex noun phrases are common in academic writing because adding modifiers is an efficient way to present information.

Noun phrase modified with an adjective and a prepositional phrase:

*The **sensitive** issue **of gender inequality** has been discussed for many decades.*

Noun phrase modified with an adjective and an identifying relative clause:

*Sometimes **professional** women **who start their own businesses** have trouble getting loans.*

2.1 Modifiers After Nouns

A Common modifiers after a noun are:

relative clauses

prepositional phrases

RELATIVE CLAUSE

*New York has the most women **who own businesses**.*

PREP. PHRASE

*The organization provides advice for women **in business**.*

B Some relative clauses can be shortened by dropping the relative pronoun and the *be* verb.

-*ing* phrases

-*ed* phrases

*The number of women ~~who are~~ **starting their own businesses** is increasing.*

*Women ~~who are~~ **elected to Congress** are in the minority.*

2.2 Using Noun Phrases

A In academic writing, complex noun phrases can often replace other parts of speech, such as verb phrases. This process makes it possible to pack information into a sentence more efficiently by reducing the number of clauses.

Writers also use complex noun phrases to connect ideas between sentences.

VERB PHRASE

*Recent research shows that there **are more mothers***

VERB PHRASE

***who are working**. (2 clauses)*

NOUN PHRASE

*Recent research shows **an increase in the number of working mothers**. (1 clause)*

*The **salary** of men and women **differ significantly** for the same job. This **significant difference** in **salary** is one indication of persistent inequality.*

2.2 Using Noun Phrases *(continued)*

B A complex noun phrase can often replace a verb (usually *be*) + adjective. The adjective from the verb phrase becomes part of the noun phrase. This makes it possible to include more information in one sentence.

VERB *BE* + ADJ.

*The rise of women in business **has been impressive**.*

This indicates that traditional gender roles are being challenged.

NOUN PHRASE

***The impressive rise of** women in business indicates that traditional gender roles are being challenged.*

C In comparison and contrast writing, noun modifiers are used to compare and contrast items in detail.

*The boy twin received a **blue blanket with white stripes**, while his twin sister received a **pink blanket with yellow stripes**.*

 Grammar Application

Exercise 2.1 Complex Noun Phrases

A Read the sentences about gender and careers. Underline the relative clauses. Circle the prepositional phrases that come after nouns.

1 A couple of decades ago, women <u>who were interested in studying engineering</u> were rare.

2 Today, there are more and more women in the field of engineering.

3 There didn't use to be many men who were attracted to the field of nursing.

4 Now the number of men who are working as nurses is growing.

5 Two fields that were once occupied only by men were law enforcement and firefighting.

6 These are two careers that are attracting many young women today.

7 Because of an increase in demand and services in data communications and home health-care aides, more men and women are choosing professions in these areas.

B Pair Work On a separate sheet of paper rewrite each sentence from A that contains a relative clause. Shorten the relative clauses to *-ed* and *-ing* phrases.

1. A couple of decades ago, women interested in studying engineering were rare.

Read each sentence or pair of sentences about women in the workplace. Next, write the words in bold as a noun phrase in the sentence that follows. Change the form of the words as necessary.

1 The number of women working outside the home has **increased significantly**.

There has been a _significant increase_ in the number of women working outside the home.

2 It has not been easy for women to **achieve progress** toward equality in the workplace.

The _______________ of _______________ toward equality in the workplace has not been easy for women.

3 The **growing** number of women in management **is recent**. This indicates that gender differences are becoming less important.

The _______________ _______________ in the number of women in management indicates that gender differences are becoming less important.

4 In many companies the **roles** of men are **dominant**. This is still evident, although it is changing.

The _______________ _______________ of men in many companies is still evident, although it is changing.

5 The **struggle** for women in the workplace has been **long** and **difficult**. This has resulted in many more career opportunities in recent years.

The _______________ and _______________ _______________ for women in the workplace has resulted in many more career opportunities in recent years.

6 Women have **increasingly participated** in the workforce; nevertheless, gender inequality continues.

Although there is an _______________ in the _______________ of women in the workforce, gender inequality continues.

7 Current research shows that the number of women going to medical school and law school is **rising steadily**. This is expected to continue.

The _______________ _______________ in the number of women going to medical school and law school is expected to continue, according to current research.

8 **Women's enrollment** in college has been **higher** than men's since 2000. This is due in part to the fact that more men drop out.

_______________ _______________ _______________ in college since 2000 is due in part to the fact that more men drop out.

9 In a recent survey, men **perceive** career advancement more **optimistically** than women. This supports the fact that men hold the majority of middle management positions.

Men's _______________ _______________ concerning career advancement supports the fact that men hold the majority of middle management positions.

3 Parallel Structure

Grammar Presentation

When each item in a list or comparison follows the same grammatical pattern, it is easier for readers to understand complex ideas. This is called *parallel structure*.

*In some cultures, men are expected to be **assertive**, **confident**, and **decisive**.*

*In some cultures, women **spend the day taking** care of the children, while **men spend the day working** outside the house.*

3.1 Parallel Structure

A Parallel structure applies to series of:

adjectives

*Boys are encouraged to be **aggressive** [ADJECTIVE], **outgoing** [ADJECTIVE], and **strong** [ADJECTIVE].*

Many Vietnamese believe that marriage should promote the

noun phrases

*interests of **the community** [NOUN PHRASE], **the family** [NOUN PHRASE], and **the couple** [NOUN PHRASE].*

verb phrases

*A Brazilian bride and groom **say their wedding vows** [VERB PHRASE],*

***kiss** [VERB PHRASE], and **exchange rings** [VERB PHRASE].*

Many women struggle with cultural expectations

clauses

***when they pursue a career** [CLAUSE] or **when they decide not to marry** [CLAUSE].*

B Items in a series are often the same length. This makes the ideas easier to understand.

*Receptions for Brazilian weddings involve **delicious food**, **much laughter**, and **constant music**. (The items listed are all about the same length – each noun is modified by one adjective.)*

C Writers often use parallel structure to compare and contrast items in a series.

*Years ago, men **worked** outside the home, while women **cleaned** the house, **did** the cooking, and **cared for** the children.*

Exercise 3.1 Parallel Structure

Choose the best answer to complete the sentences about gender differences below.

1 Men and women working together can reduce inequality slowly, carefully, and *significantly* .
   a with significance   b significantly   c significant

2 Unlike the past, these days women are often encouraged to go to college, have careers,
   and ___________________ .
   a invests in her future   b investing in their future   c invest in their future

3 Both men and women enjoy going to work, making money, and ___________________ .
   a provides for their families   b providing for their families   c they provide for their families

4 Traditionally, men have often been encouraged to become competitive, aggressive,
   and ___________________ .
   a unemotional   b they are not emotional   c they can't show their feelings

5 Companies that attract women tend to offer opportunities for advancement, flexible
   schedules, and ___________________ .
   a they have mentors for them   b mentors   c women need mentors

6 Unlike women, men are much more likely to ask for raises, bonuses, and ___________________ .
   a promote   b promoting   c promotions

Exercise 3.2 More Parallel Structure

A Write answers to the questions below about men, women, and careers, using parallel
structure. Use your own ideas or ideas that you have learned in this unit.

1 What are three things that women can do to decrease gender inequality in the workplace?
   Women can refuse to accept unfair treatment, make men more aware of
   their behavior, and continue to ask for what they want.

2 What are three skills that many people thought in the past were women's skills?

3 What are two professions that men typically did in the past that are now also done
   by women?

4 What are three careers that women have traditionally gone into?

5 What are two different ways that some women react to having a female boss?

6 What are two possible ways that women are different from men in relationships?

B Write answers to the questions about men, using parallel structure. Use your own ideas.

1 What are three things that men can do to decrease gender inequality in the workplace?

   Men can be more aware of their behavior, honest in their interactions, and accepting of women as their equals.

2 What are three skills that many people believe are more suited to men than women? Why do you think most people have this belief?

3 What are three professions that women did in the past that are now also done by men? What are your feelings about having men in these professions?

4 What are two professions that people still associate with men rather than women? What are possible reasons for this?

5 In your experience, what are two ways that some men react to having a female boss?

6 In your opinion, do men in their 20s and 30s have different perceptions of women in the workplace than men who are older? Why or why not? Give two reasons for your opinion.

C Group Work Share your ideas for each item in A and B in a group. Tell if you agree or disagree and why.

A *I say that women can refuse to accept unfair treatment, make men more aware of their behavior, and continue to ask for what they want. Those behaviors would decrease gender inequality.*

B *I don't agree with everything you say because first of all, I think that management must change and that change is difficult because it is like changing a culture's values and ideas.*

Men, Women, and Equality   **87**

4 Common Quantifiers 🌐

Vocabulary Presentation

Quantifiers indicate the amount or degree of something. They can help a writer be more precise and avoid overgeneralizations. They are common in comparison and contrast academic writing.

Many top positions are filled by men.

Few of the top executives are women.

4.1 Quantifiers

A Quantifiers are used before nouns. Examples include: *all, almost all, both, few, most, no, several, some*.

Most toys are gender-specific.

Several women hold important positions in that company.

B Quantifiers also follow the pattern:

quantifier + of +:
the / this / that / these / those / such +
noun phrase
possessive pronoun (*my, your*, etc.) + noun phrase
object pronoun (*it, them, us*, etc.)

Note: Use *none* instead of *no* in this pattern.

Many of the women in my country have two jobs.

Most of my friends are aware of traditional gender roles.

None of us supports inequality in the workplace.

C Use these quantifiers only before count nouns: *a few, a great many, both, few, many, several*.

Only a few presidents of countries are women.

Both boys and girls learn gender roles from an early age.

Use these quantifiers only before noncount nouns: *a great deal of, a little, little, much*.

The article contained *a great deal of* information about gender roles.

We have achieved *little* progress in gender equality.

D Some quantifiers compare amounts: *fewer, less*, and *more*.

Fewer men than women work as nurses.

Adverbs such as *considerably, significantly, slightly*, and *substantially* are common before the comparative quantifiers.

In the past, many men felt women could not succeed as executives. *Significantly fewer* men today believe that.
In the 1970s, most lawyers were men. Today there are *substantially more* female lawyers.

E Use quantifiers to change overly general statements into qualified, more precise statements in comparison and contrast writing.

Men are aggressive, and women are passive. (Too general)

Some men are dominant and *some* women are passive. (More accurate)

Vocabulary Application

Exercise 4.1 Common Quantifiers

A The graph below shows the percentage of males and females across some of the major occupational groups in Canada. Write sentences by referring to the graph and using the cues in parentheses.

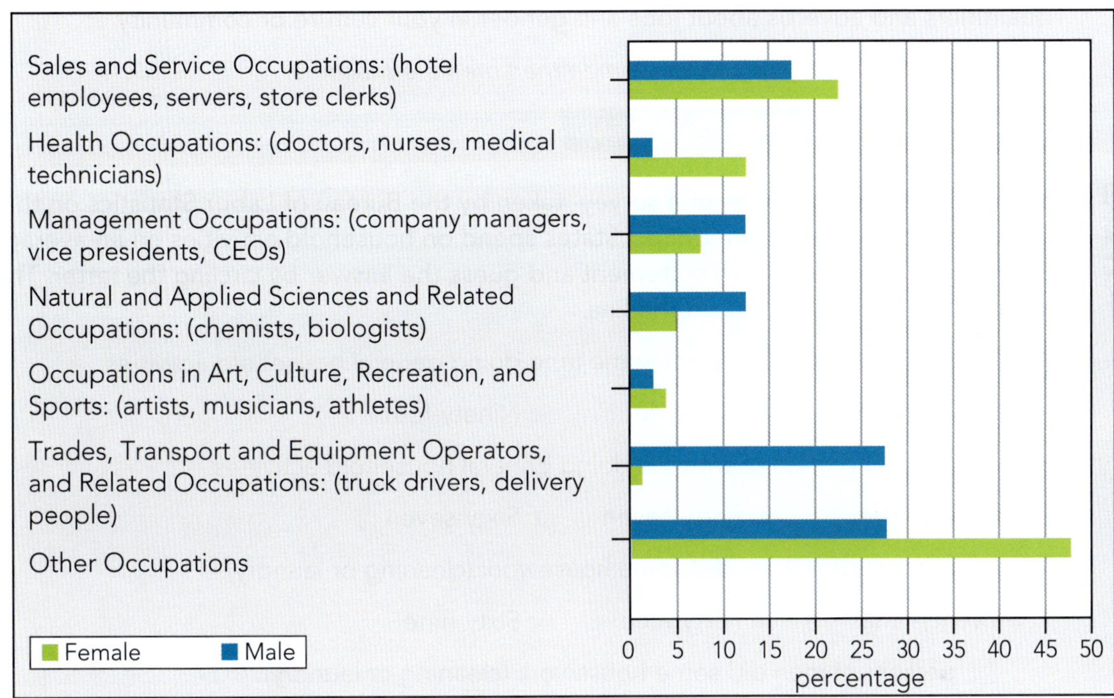

Source: Statistics Canada, Labour Force Survey. (www.statcan.gc.ca)

a great deal of	most of	a slightly higher number of
fewer	significantly fewer	substantially more

1   _A great deal of_   men are in the trades and transport areas.

2   _________________ men are in management occupations than in sales and service occupations.

3   There are _________________ men than women who are chemists and biologists.

4   _________________ women have occupations such as artists, musicians, and athletes than those of truck drivers and delivery people.

5   _________________ women than men have jobs in the trades, transport, and equipment operators sector.

6   _________________ the women have jobs in occupations not listed in the chart.

B Pair Work Work with a partner. Create three sentences using the information in the chart in A. Use the words in the box in A and other quantifiers. Share them with another pair and give a possible explanation for the statement. Do they agree with the statements?

Significantly fewer men are in health occupations. I think this may be because there are usually more women in health-care occupations such as nursing.

C Pair Work Using your own knowledge and experience, write four sentences using quantifiers and adverbs about jobs and gender in your culture or community.

In my culture, significantly more women than men are teachers.

Exercise 4.2 More Common Quantifiers

A You will listen to the results of a survey taken by the Bureau of Labor Statistics on the time that men and women in the United States spend on household activities on an average day. Before you listen, read each statement and guess the answer by circling the letter. Then listen and write the correct letter on the line.

1 _____ percent of women spent some time doing general household activities.

   a Seventy-four   b Eighty-four   c Ninety-four

2 _____ percent of men spent time doing general household activities.

   a Twenty-seven   b Forty-seven   c Sixty-seven

3 _____ percent of women did some housework (cleaning or laundry).

   a Twenty-nine   b Forty-nine   c Sixty-nine

4 _____ percent of men did some housework (cleaning or laundry).

   a Five   b Ten   c Twenty

5 _____ percent of women prepared the food and cleaned up.

   a Fifty-eight   b Sixty-eight   c Seventy-eight

6 _____ percent of men prepared food and cleaned up.

   a Twenty-one   b Thirty-one   c Forty-one

Source: www.bls.gov

B Compare the statistics in A. Write statements using the quantifiers in parentheses.

1 (significantly fewer) *Significantly fewer men than women spent time doing housework.*

2 (substantially more) ____

3 (some) ____

4 (most) ____

5 (both) ____

5 Avoid Common Mistakes ⚠ 

1   Remember to use parallel structure with two or more adjectives.

A study showed that elementary school teachers discriminated against children

inattentive

who were noisy, active, and ~~if they did not pay attention~~.

2   Remember to use parallel structure with two or more noun phrases.

Wedding guests include the friends of the bride, the bride's co-workers,
and the bride's family ~~is also invited~~.

3   Remember to use parallel structure with two or more verb phrases.

to run

The girls loved to play basketball, to wrestle, and ~~running~~ races, just like the boys.

4   Remember to use parallel structure with two or more clauses.

These days most married women feel that they should continue working,
have their own bank accounts, and ~~to~~ share household chores with their husbands.

Editing Task

Find and correct nine more mistakes in this body paragraph from an essay comparing women's roles in the past and in the present.

Women's Roles, Past and Present

Roles for women in the United States have changed in terms of the subjects that

the careers that they choose

women study in college and ~~they choose careers~~. Before the 1970s, most middle-class

men were expected to attend college and pursuing careers that were both professional

and they paid well. Men provided the main financial support for the family. Middle-class

5   women, however, were expected to get married or, if they went to college, preparing

for traditionally female professions, such as teaching or to be a nurse. Women were not

expected to support a family. If a woman worked after college, she was expected to stop

as soon as she got married or to have children. Because they did not expect to support a

family or working for a long time, some women also studied non-career-oriented subjects

10   such as literature or art history. Nowadays, in contrast, most women plan to work for most

of their adult lives and they help support their families. Many women feel that they should

prepare for a job, that they should move forward in their careers, and to find satisfaction

in their work. Therefore, today, there are many more women studying career-oriented

subjects such as business, accounting, and to work in law enforcement. In fact, many fields

15   that were once thought of as for men only, such as law enforcement, now employ women.

Although women still do not earn as much as men, they have come a long way since the

1970s in expanding their college and career opportunities.

6 Academic Writing

In this section, you will write an outline and one body paragraph for a comparison and contrast essay using the point-by-point method of organization. Before you start writing, you will learn how to write effective body paragraphs with different types of supporting details.

About Supporting Details

Topic sentences introduce the main idea of a body paragraph. In academic writing, each body paragraph must also include supporting details – often two or three details or examples that explain, or "support," the main idea of the paragraph. The following are four examples that show different ways to support the topic sentence that follows:

Topic sentence: *There have been dramatic shifts for women and girls in sports over the past four decades.*

1 **An example:** *There have been numerous professional sports leagues created for women, such as professional women's basketball and soccer leagues.*

2 **A definition:** *In the United States, Title IX refers to a major law passed in 1972 that prohibited discrimination against women and girls in school-based sports.*

3 **A historical fact:** *In 1972, the passage of Title IX required equal funding for girls' sports.*

4 **Statistical data:** *Prior to Title IX, the ratio of boys to girls participating in sports in schools was over 27 to 1; it is now almost equal.*

There are other ways to support a topic sentence, such as providing a description, making comparisons, or explaining causes and effects. As a writer, you must decide what types of details will best support the main ideas of your body paragraphs.

Exercise

A Match the parts of an essay on the right with the corresponding example of it on the left.
Write the letter of the example on the line.

<table>
<tr>
<td>

_______ **1** Thesis statement

_______ **2** Body paragraph 1: Topic
sentence

_______ **3** A supporting detail for
body paragraph 1

_______ **4** Body paragraph 2: Topic
sentence

_______ **5** A supporting detail for
body paragraph 2

_______ **6** Body paragraph 3: Topic
sentence

_______ **7** A supporting detail for
body paragraph 3

</td>
<td>

a The first major shift has been the increase in the
commercialization of sports.

b Since the 1980s, professional basketball and
soccer leagues for women have been formed,
creating opportunities for women to earn money
playing the sports that they love and excel at.

c The seasons for many sports have gotten longer,
and athletes often train all year with professional
trainers.

d Commercialization refers to the focus on selling
the product and making a profit.

e Over the past 50 years, sports in the United
States have become more commercial,
competitive, and gender-neutral.

f Another big change has been the rise of women
in sports.

g As sports have become big businesses, athletes
at all levels have trained and played with more
intensity.

</td>
</tr>
</table>

B Look at your answers in A for items 3, 5, and 7, and write the type of supporting detail for
each one: *an example*, *a definition*, or *a historical fact*.

1 The supporting detail for item 3 is _____________________ .

2 The supporting detail for item 5 is _____________________ .

3 The supporting detail for item 7 is _____________________ .

Pre-writing Tasks
Choose a Topic

A Choose one of the essay topics below. You will write one body paragraph for a comparison
and contrast essay on this topic. Your body paragraph will use the point-by-point method.

- One aspect of society (sports, business, family) in two different cultures
- One aspect of society (sports, business, family) 50 years ago and now
- A topic approved by your teacher

B Pair Work Share your topic with a partner. Describe the points that you will compare and contrast. Give your partner suggestions about supporting points (comparisons, definitions, examples, facts, etc.) to include.

Organize Your Ideas

A Follow the steps below to develop and organize your ideas before you write.

1 In Unit 5, you outlined a comparison and contrast essay that used the block method. With that method, all the main points and details for one side of an issue are presented together in one "block," and the same main points for the second side of the issue are presented in a second "block."

2 Now outline an essay, using the point-by-point method in which both sides of the first point are presented, then both sides of the second point are presented, and so on. Use the outline in the left column below for an essay on gender inequality to help you complete a point-by-point outline for your topic in the right column.

Title: "Gender Inequality"	Title:
I **Introductory Paragraph** **Thesis Statement:** Gender inequality and differences can still be found in the workplace as well as in cultural and social aspects of American life.	**I** **Introductory Paragraph** **Thesis Statement:**
II **Body Paragraph 1** – Point 1: Gender role in the workplace **Supporting Details:** ■ Men's role in the workplace ■ Women's role in the workplace	**II** **Body Paragraph 1** – Point 1: **Supporting Details:** ■ ■
III **Body Paragraph 2** – Point 2: Gender role in the home **Supporting Details:** ■ Men's role in the home ■ Women's role in the home	**III** **Body Paragraph 2** – Point 2: **Supporting Details:** ■ ■
IV **Body Paragraph 3** – Point 3: Gender role in society **Supporting Details:** ■ Men's role in society ■ Women's role in society	**IV** **Body Paragraph 3** – Point 3: **Supporting Details:** ■ ■
V **Conclusion**	**V** **Conclusion**

B Pair Work Share your outline with a partner and discuss your ideas.

Writing Task

Write one of the body paragraphs from your outline. Follow the steps below.

1 Include a topic sentence and two or three supporting details about the specific point of comparison or contrast.

Academic Writing Tip

Avoid Using the Quantifiers *A Lot Of* and *Lots Of*

The quantifiers *a lot of* and *lots of* are informal expressions. Use *many* or *a great deal of* instead.

2 Include the following in your paragraph:

- complex noun phrases;

- sentences using parallel structure;

- a variety of modifiers;

- at least three of these academic words from the essay in this unit: *adult, approximately, aspect, cooperative, corporation, create, cultural, culture, decade, despite, dominant, environment, financial, flexible, gender, interaction, job, legal, major, majority, reinforce, role, significant, subordinate.*

3 After you write your paragraph, review it and make sure that you avoided the mistakes in the Avoid Common Mistakes chart on page 91.

Peer Review

A Exchange your outline and paragraph with a partner. Answer the following questions as you read your partner's outline and paragraph, and then share your responses.

1 Is the outline organized using the point-by-point method?

2 Do the supporting sentences adequately support the topic sentence?

3 Are there any noun phrases? Are the sentences with those noun phrases easy to understand? Explain.

4 Are there any sentences that use parallel structure? If not, make suggestions for places to include one or more.

5 Are quantifiers used to make comparisons between main ideas? Suggest other quantifiers if you feel the comparisons overgeneralize.

6 Is anything confusing? Write a question mark (?) next to it.

7 Provide one compliment (something you found interesting or unusual).

B Use your partner's comments to help you revise your paragraph. Use the Writer's Checklist on page A2 to review your paragraph for organization, grammar, and vocabulary.

Comparison and Contrast 3: Comparative and Superlative Adjectives and Adverbs; Articles; Common Expressions That Show Similarity

Family Values in Different Cultures

1 Grammar in the Real World

You will read an essay about cultural differences between U.S. families from two cultural backgrounds: Latino and traditional U.S. The essay is an example of one kind of comparison and contrast writing in which the writer compares and contrasts aspects of two cultures.

A Before You Read What does the term *family* mean to you? Read the essay. What are some ways that the writer defines *family*?

B Comprehension Check Answer the questions.

1 How are the beliefs of Dr. Benjamin Spock related to the way many U.S. families raise their children?

2 Who might young Latino adults live with when they finish college? What about college graduates in traditional U.S. families?

3 What does the writer mean by "it is wise not to stereotype cultures"? Do you think the writer avoids stereotyping cultures in this essay? Explain.

C Notice Answer the questions below to help you notice the use of comparative adjectives and other ways to describe differences and similarities.

1 Reread lines 24–25 in the second paragraph. What did Dr. Spock believe American children should become as they got older? Notice the two forms of the comparative. What determines which form is used?

2 What two things does the writer compare on lines 44–50?

3 Reread the last paragraph. How are traditional U.S. and Latino cultures the same? Underline the words the writer uses to show similarity.

D Academic Writing When you summarize, you write the most important points and information of a paragraph or reading in your own words. Summarize paragraph 2. Compare your summary with your classmate's.

What Family Means:
An Intercultural Perspective

THE DEFINITION OF FAMILY differs from culture to culture. These differences become more apparent when families
5 from diverse cultures live in the same area. For example, with the increasing number of Latinos in the United States, diversity in the culture of
10 U.S. families has become more noticeable. Differences include how family is defined, how children view themselves within the family, and what happens when children reach young adulthood.

15 Traditionally, in U.S. culture, when people refer to their family, they usually mean their immediate family, that is, their parents and their children. Many of these families follow the basic principles of Dr. Benjamin Spock, a famous pediatrician[1] in the mid-
20 1900s. He wrote a popular book on raising children that changed the style of parenting from strict to more permissive. He believed that children should be free to set their own goals and choose their own career path. In Dr. Spock's view, as children
25 get older they should become more independent (Dr. Spock, n.d., para. 4). After finishing high school, American teenagers who go to college often move out of their parents' homes and live in a college dormitory or their own apartment. After college,
30 many live on their own. Children who continue to live with their parents after high school or college might be asked to pay rent. In general, family takes on a smaller role as children enter adulthood.

In contrast, in many Latino cultures, when
35 people refer to their family, they include extended family, such as aunts, uncles, cousins, and grandparents. Latino life centers on family. In fact, the largest component of Latino life is usually the family. Sociologists have suggested that
40 each family member feels a moral responsibility to help other members of the family who may be experiencing problems such as poor health, financial concerns, and unemployment (Clutter & Nieto, 2009, p. 1). It is common for Latino families
45 to encourage longer visits from relatives, and they expect loyalty, sacrifice, and hard work from family members. Many Latino young adults live with their parents until marriage, and in some cases even after marriage. This is seen as more acceptable in
50 Latino culture than in traditional US culture.

Beliefs about family relationships and expectations differ among traditional U.S. and Latino cultures. Despite these differences, traditional U.S. culture is similar to Latino culture in
55 terms of the importance of family. Understanding the cultural background of others is valuable for people living in diverse communities, like in the United States. However, it is wise not to stereotype cultures. Not all Latino families stick
60 together. Similarly, not all parents from traditional U.S. culture point to the door when their children turn 18. Cultural background plays a role in our relationships with family members, but culture is rarely the sole defining element for anyone.

---

[1]**pediatrician:** a doctor who treats children

2 Comparative and Superlative Adjectives and Adverbs

Grammar Presentation

Comparatives show how two things or ideas are different. Superlatives compare one thing or idea to others in a group. They are both important in comparison and contrast writing.

*In general, Asians are **less relaxed** about time **than** Latinos.*

*The **largest component** of Latino life is the family.*

*In general, sports fans in Latin America follow soccer **more intensely than** baseball.*

*People from traditional U.S. culture communicate **the most directly**.*

2.1 Comparative Adjectives and Adverbs

A Comparative adjectives are formed as follows:

Add *-er* to one-syllable and some two-syllable adjectives: *easier, greater, older.*

Add *more / less* before adjectives with two or more syllables: *more complex, less efficient.*

*Mexicans often have **larger** families **than** Chinese.*

*The concept of family is **easier** to define in some cultures **than** in others.*

*The extended family is **more important** in Latino families **than** in some other cultures.*

*The concept of family in the United States is **less rigid than** in other cultures.*

B Comparative adverbs are formed as follows:

Add *-er* to one-syllable and some two-syllable adverbs: *earlier, harder, faster.*

Add *more / less* before adverbs of two syllables or more: *more quickly, less carefully.*

*Children from traditional U.S. culture usually leave home **earlier than** children in Latino culture.*

*Some people talk **more quickly than** others.*

*In general, the Japanese treat the elderly **more respectfully**.*

C Do not use *less* with one-syllable words. Use *not as . . . as.*

*The Asian population is **not as** large **as** the Latino population in the United States.*

NOT *The Asian population is ~~less large than~~ the Latino population in the United States.*

D Use a subject pronoun + an auxiliary verb (*be*, *have*, or *do*) after than in formal academic writing. The auxiliary verb is optional.

Use an object pronoun in informal writing and speaking.

FORMAL: *My family is more concerned about having dinner together **than I (am)**.*

INFORMAL: *My family is more concerned about having dinner together **than me**.*

2.2 Superlative Adjectives and Adverbs

A Superlative adjectives are formed as follows:

Add *the + -est* to one-syllable and some two-syllable adjectives: *easiest, greatest, oldest*.

Add *the most/the least* before adjectives with two or more syllables: *most common, least effective*.

*Latinos are currently one of **the largest** ethnic groups in the United States.*

*Solidarity is **the most significant** value for people of my culture.*

B Superlative adverbs are formed as follows:

Add *the + -est* to one-syllable adverbs: *hardest, fastest*.

Add *the most* before adverbs of two or more syllables: *the most quickly, the most significantly*.

*Researchers often debate about which groups work **the hardest**.*

*The Latino population in the United States has increased **the most significantly** of all ethnic groups in the country.*

2.3 Using Comparatives

A There are two common uses of comparatives:
Explicit: Both elements to be compared are included in the sentence.

COMPARED ITEM 1
*Independence is **more valued** in the United States than*

COMPARED ITEM 2
in other cultures.

COMPARED ITEM 1   COMPARED ITEM 2
*My sister and I are close, but my brother and I are **closer**.*

B Implicit: The comparison is with something already mentioned in the text, or with something outside the text but known to the reader. As a result, it is not necessary to repeat "*than* + the second element" after the verb.

*If people from traditional U.S. culture knew more about other cultures, they perhaps would be **more understanding** (than they are).*

DATA FROM THE REAL WORLD

In academic writing, comparatives with *-er* are more common than superlatives with *-est*. Writers tend to avoid making strong claims. Common adjectives include: *best, better, earlier, easier, greater, greatest, higher, highest, larger, largest, lower, older, smaller, wider*

*The number of immigrants is **higher** in the United States than in Canada.*

Exercise 2.1 Comparative Adjectives and Adverbs

A Read each sentence or pair of sentences about traditional U.S. culture. Then complete the second sentence that is a restatement of the information. Use the comparative form of the adjective or adverb in parentheses. Include *than* when necessary.

1 Children from traditional U.S. culture are very assertive, compared to children from some other cultures.

   Children from traditional U.S. culture are _more assertive than_ (assertive) children from some other cultures.

2 Parents from traditional U.S. culture often allow their teenage children to work while they are in school. Parents from some other cultures want their children to focus only on education until they are out of school.

   Parents from other cultures are much ________________ (likely) parents from traditional U.S. culture to allow their children to work while they are in school.

3 Children from traditional U.S. culture are often permitted to stay out late on weekends. Parents from some other cultures do not allow their children to stay out late.

   Parents from traditional U.S. culture behave ________________ (strictly) parents from some other cultures.

4 Children from traditional U.S. culture speak informally to their elders. Children in most Asian families speak politely to their elders.

   Children in most Asian families speak ________________ (politely) to their elders.

5 In traditional U.S. culture, elderly parents don't often live with their grown children like they do in other cultures.

   While in many cultures elderly parents often live with their grown children, this is much ________________ (common) in traditional U.S. culture.

6 In many cultures, grandparents help to raise their grandchildren. This is not normally the case in traditional U.S. culture.

   When it comes to their grandchildren's upbringing, grandparents from other cultures are often ________________ (involved) grandparents in traditional U.S. culture.

7 In traditional U.S. culture, the concept of family usually means parents and their children. In other cultures, *family* can mean parents, their children, the children's grandparents, and sometimes aunts, uncles, and cousins.

   In traditional U.S. culture, the concept of family is ________________ (complex) in other cultures.

B Pair Work Work with a partner. Compare each statement in A to another culture that you are familiar with. Use words from the Data from the Real World chart as necessary. When you are finished, report your ideas to the class.

I would say that Japanese children are less assertive than children from traditional U.S. culture because in Japanese culture it is more desirable to be part of a group.

Exercise 2.2 Superlative Adjectives and Adverbs

Complete the sentences with your ideas about cultural behaviors. Use the superlative forms of the adjectives and adverbs in parentheses.

1 One of _the biggest_ (big) differences between my culture and _traditional U.S._ culture is _the way children speak to their parents_ .

2 I think _________________________ (important) thing to know about my culture is

_________________________ .

3 The _________________________ (strange) thing I ever learned about a different

culture is _________________________ .

4 I think _________________________ (difficult) thing to understand about

_________________________ culture is _________________________ .

5 The _________________________ (significantly) different thing between my culture

and _________________________ culture is _________________________ .

6 The person in my family who works _________________________ (hard) is

_________________________ .

7 The person in my family who behaves _________________________ (patiently) is

_________________________ .

A Listen to the lecture about ways that cultures differ. As you listen, check (✓) the correct columns in the chart.

		High-Context	Low-Context	Collectivist	Individualist
1	Communication is direct.		✓		
2	Communication is indirect.				
3	Tone of voice, gestures, and status are important.				
4	The United States and European countries are examples of this type.				
5	Japan and South Korea are examples of this type.				
6	Africa, Latin America, and Asia are examples of this type.				
7	The group is valued.				
8	Family ties are strong.				
9	Merit and expertise are important.				
10	A person's goals are important.				

B Complete the sentences about cultural behaviors with comparatives or superlatives. Use the information from the chart in A and the adjective or adverb form of the words in parentheses. Include *than* when necessary.

1 There are a lot of important things to consider when working with people of different cultures. However, one of ___*the most important*___ (important) topics to learn about is communication style.

2 In high-context cultures like South Korea and Japan, the communication style is ___________________________ (direct) that of people in low-context cultures.

3 In low-context cultures like the United States and England, people communicate ___________________________ (direct).

4 For people in high-context cultures, words are not the only tool of communication. In low-context cultures, words are ___________________________ (essential) thing.

5 Facial expressions, gestures, and tone of voice are often ___________________________ (important) in low-context cultures.

6 Degree of individualism is one of ________________________ (big) issues to consider when observing cultural differences.

7 In collectivist cultures, the group is valued ________________________ (high) it is in individualistic cultures.

8 In individualistic cultures, an individual's goals are ________________________ (valued) a group's goals.

9 Collectivist cultures consider a person's merit or expertise ________________________ (important) family ties.

10 Communicating effectively with people from other cultures can be difficult. That's why ________________________ (critical) important thing to do is to learn about cultural differences beforehand.

3 Articles

Grammar Presentation

Articles (*a/an, the*) or no article (Ø) precede nouns. Articles help writers distinguish between general and specific statements and shared knowledge. This is important in academic writing, including in comparison and contrast writing.

*In Latin America, Ø families include **a** mother, **a** father, Ø sisters, Ø brothers, Ø aunts, Ø uncles, and Ø cousins.*

*I have not met **the** family that lives across **the** street from my house.*

3.1 Using the Definite Article

A Use *the* when both the writer and the reader share common knowledge or information about the noun.

*In many cultures, it is important for families to eat meals together in **the** kitchen.* (The writer assumes the reader shares the knowledge that there is usually one kitchen in a house.)

B Use *the* when the noun was introduced earlier in the text and you give more information, or when the noun is related to a noun mentioned earlier.

*Each person in a family has a moral responsibility to aid other members of **the** family experiencing financial problems.*

C Use *the* when you are writing about "which one" (when there is additional information that identifies the specific noun).

Mexico is **the** country that is located south of the United States.

D Use *the* with superlatives.

The strictest family I ever met was from the United States.

E Use *the* for:

abbreviations

(but usually not for acronyms)

groups

adjectives that refer to a category

when there is only one

the CIA, **the** UN, **the** FBI

Ø NASA, Ø NATO

the media, **the** military

the rich, **the** elderly

the president, **the** queen, **the** United States, **the** Alps, **the** moon, **the** equator

3.2 Using the Indefinite Article

A Use *a / an* with a singular count noun when the noun is not specifically identified, or when it is first mentioned and new to the reader.

A young Latino man is the new student in class. (The man is not specifically identified.)

The class read **an** article about cultural values. (The reader does not know this article.)

B Do not use *a / an* with noncount or plural nouns. Use *some* or Ø.

My cousin borrowed **some money** from me, but he has not paid me back yet.

Ø Large **families** can be enjoyable but complicated.

C Use *a / an* when introducing a count noun.

A young Latina woman is the new student in my class. I found out that she is from Colombia.

3.3 Using Articles in Discourse

A In academic writing, paragraphs and essays often begin with generalizations. Use the indefinite article when making generalizations:

Ø for noncount nouns and plural nouns

a / an for singular nouns

"Ø Advertising is about Ø norms and Ø values, Ø aspirations and Ø prejudices." –Anil Ambani

*In some cultures, **a** teenager is expected to move out of their parents' home and live in **a** college dormitory.*

B Use the definite article if it refers to a specific noun that is known to the reader. The reference may be:

direct

*Teens leave their parents' homes to live in a dormitory. **The** parents are often sad to see their children leave. (Parents were already mentioned.)*

clear from context

*Although **the** rooms are often very small, most teenagers do not seem to mind. (Readers know that dormitories have rooms.)*

Grammar Application

Exercise 3.1 Indefinite and Definite Articles

A Read the article about how relationships are affected by mobility in the United States. Choose the best article (*a / an*, *the*, or Ø) for each item. Sometimes more than one answer is possible.

Mobility in the United States

The United States is a very mobile society. People frequently do not live in the same town for their entire lives. Often ____Ø____ (1) large corporations require their employees to move if they want to advance in __________ (2) company. Students typically do not go to __________ (3) college near their families. As a result, it is not uncommon for __________ (4) extended families to be separated by hundreds, if not thousands, of miles.

This mobility is probably one of __________ (5) most significant factors influencing __________ (6) relationships in the United States. For example, people tend to be very friendly on a casual basis and open to meeting

many new individuals, but these interactions do not always result

in __________ close, lasting relationships. There is __________
        (7)   (8)
common tendency of people in __________ United States to say
                               (9)
things like, "Let's get together sometime," or "Let's have lunch,"

and then not follow through with __________ invitation.
                                   (10)
    People who are not from __________ United States
                           (11)
sometimes see this informal style as superficial, and it can be

confusing. If someone says, "Let's get together," __________
                                                      (12)
visitor to the United States might expect the person to make

__________ call and suggest __________ meeting time and place.
   (13)   (14)
This doesn't always happen. However, __________ visitor who has this experience
                                        (15)
shouldn't be offended because __________ expression "Let's get together" has almost
                                (16)
__________ same meaning as "hello" to many Americans.
   (17)

B Group Work Take turns explaining why you chose each answer in A.

*I chose no article for item 1 because corporations is plural and here the writer is
referring to all large corporations, not specific large corporations.*

Exercise 3.2 More Indefinite and Definite Articles

A Write sentences about cultural differences with the cues in parentheses. Use your own ideas.
Use the correct articles.

1 (a definition of *family*) *A family can consist of parents and children, or it can
  consist of parents, children, grandparents, and others.*

2 (a definition of *values*) ____

____

3 (a generalization about cultural differences – what they are) _______________

____

4 (a description of one cultural difference concerning time, family, relationships, etc.)

____

____

5 (a detail about your difference in item 4) _________________________________

____

6 (a statement about a cultural difference that you think is more confusing than any other)

____

7 (a generalization about groups and individuals in your culture) _______________

____

B Pair Work Talk with a partner about your sentences in A. Which sentences are generalizations? Which contain specific nouns? Share your sentences with another pair. Ask the other pair to identify the reason why each article or no article is appropriate.

You used "a family" in this sentence because here you are using a singular count noun to make a generalization.

4 Common Expressions That Show Similarity 🌐

Vocabulary Presentation

Some words and phrases are commonly used to show similarity in comparison and contrast writing.	*There are many **similarities** between Turkish and Brazilian cultures.* *Japanese and South Koreans **have something in common**: they tend to avoid directly looking into someone's eyes while speaking.*

4.1 Similar to, Similarities, Similarly, Likewise, Like

A Use *be similar to* to compare two noun phrases.	*Mexican culture **is similar to** Spanish culture in many ways.*
B Use *the similarities between ______ and ______* to compare two noun phrases.	*Many people believe that **the similarities between** the United States **and** Canada outweigh the differences.*
C Use *similarly* and *likewise* as transition words to connect sentences with shared features. Use a comma after the words.	*In Nigeria, social recognition is achieved through extended families. **Similarly,** a family's honor is influenced by the action of its members.* *Chinese children enjoy playing video games. **Likewise,** American children find this an enjoyable activity.*

D Use _____ and _____ have + something/ one thing/a lot + in common to introduce shared features of two nouns.	*Germany* **and** *Spain* **have something in common**: *their people love coffee.*
E Use *Like* _____, before a clause to show how a noun is similar in one way to the subject of the clause.	*Like* *bedtime stories in the United States, the stories that Chinese parents tell their children send a strong message about values.*

Vocabulary Application

Exercise 4.1 Words That Show Similarity

A Complete the sentences about culture and online media with the appropriate word or expression from the box. Use each word or expression only once.

in common	like	similarities between
is similar to	~~likewise~~	similarly

1 A person who does business with people from different cultures should be aware of how cultures differ in communication styles. __*Likewise*__, website designers should be aware of how people from different cultures will respond to their designs.

2 People from different cultures communicate in different ways, but most have one important thing __________________ . People in most cultures use the Internet on a daily basis.

3 Years ago, there were many __________________ paper-based media and online media. Both included simple text and images that people read from top to bottom. Now, however, online media is much more interactive.

4 __________________ a person engaging in face-to-face communication, a website designer must take into account another person's expectations and assumptions. Some users may expect direct communication, while others may want more indirect messages.

5 In terms of cultural expectations, face-to-face interaction __________________ Internet interaction. Some cultures may expect a website to communicate information directly with headlines and clear text. Others may respond better to less text and more images.

6 In some cultures, the relationship between speakers is important in face-to-face communication. __________________ some Internet users may respond better to websites that have animation or interactivity that imitates human interaction.

B Pair Work With a partner, think of other ways that face-to-face communication and online communication are similar. On a separate sheet of paper, write five sentences using the expressions in A. Next, trade papers with another pair. Read their sentences. Share examples that illustrate their ideas.

5 Avoid Common Mistakes ⚠

1 Remember to use *more* or *-er* in comparisons. Do not use both.
Middle Eastern families tend to be ~~more~~ closer than families in other cultures.

2 Remember to use *best*, not *most*, before nouns.

In the 1960s, the ~~most~~-selling child-rearing book in the U.S. was Raising an Independent Child. (best)

3 Do not use the definite article *the* with title/position + name.
~~The~~ Dr. Benjamin Spock wrote Baby and Child Care in 1946.

4 Remember to use *the* in the expression *the same as.*

Child-rearing beliefs in one culture are rarely ⌄ *same as child-rearing beliefs in another culture.* (the)

Editing Task

Find and correct eight more mistakes in the body paragraphs from an essay comparing the celebration of the new year in different cultures.

Women's Roles, Past and Present

The celebration of the New Year in South Korea is not ⌄ same as in the United States. (the)
First of all, South Koreans celebrate the Lunar New Year (the second new moon in winter),
so the date is not same as in the United States, where the New Year is celebrated on
the first day of the Gregorian Calendar (January 1). The New Year is more later in South

5   Korea, usually in February. In addition, the South Korean New Year celebration lasts for
three days and involves the entire family. According to the Dr. Sook-Bin Woo, this is
because South Korean families tend to be more closer than traditional U.S. families. For
example, South Korean families play special games with each other during this holiday.
This family closeness may be the reason that many South Koreans report that their most

10   childhood memories are of New Year's celebrations.

In the United States, the celebration of the New Year begins on the evening of the
last day of the year and continues into the following day; it is therefore more shorter than
the South Korean celebration. Traditionally, it tends to be primarily an adult celebration
for many people. On New Year's Eve, many adults hire a babysitter for their children

15   and go out to a restaurant or to a party to celebrate with other adults. Because U.S.
celebrations often do not include children, most Americans are unlikely to say that their
most childhood memories are of the celebration of the New Year. Sociologist the Dr.
George Lee notes that this tradition is changing in the United States as more adults stay
home and celebrate with their children.

6 Academic Writing

In this section, you will write a comparison and contrast essay using either the point-by-point or the block method. You will use information from outside sources to make your essay stronger. Before you start writing, you will learn about summarizing.

About Summarizing

When academic writers support their ideas, they often include information and ideas by experts to sound convincing. They will not want to include everything that was written or said, so they summarize the information. The following is a summary of the essay "What Family Means: An Intercultural Perspective" on page 97 of this unit with guidelines for summarizing appropriately and effectively.

1 Identify the source of the information. Use reporting verbs.

2 Include all the main ideas from the text. The main ideas are in **bold**.

3 Omit less important ideas and specific details that are not really necessary.

4 Use paraphrasing strategies. For original text, see the essay on page 97.

5 Do not include your own ideas when summarizing.

6 Do not add any new information that is not in the text.

In the text "What Family Means: An Intercultural Perspective," Smith (2012) **points out** that the United States and many Latino cultures have different concepts of family. First, **the definition of family is different.** In the United States, *immediate family* refers

5 to parents and children, while in many Latino cultures, *immediate family* includes grandparents, uncles, aunts, and cousins. **Family expectations are also different in the two cultures.** In Latino cultures, most children are expected to live with their parents until they get married. ~~I believe this can bring many problems to the~~

10 ~~family dynamic.~~ They are also expected to take care of their family members when they are sick or when they need help. In contrast, in the United States, children are raised to be more independent. After high school, most teenagers are expected to get a job and support themselves. ~~Once a person has graduated, they might be~~

15 ~~expected to pay rent if they live at home.~~ The concept of extended family does not play as big of a role in the United States as it does in Latino cultures. ~~Also, in Latino cultures, people tend to get married at a much younger age than in the United States.~~ Even though it is beneficial to understand cultural differences and expectations,

20 it is important to bear in mind that culture is only one factor in determining the dynamics of a family.

Exercise

A Interview someone about the differences between two cultures that he or she is familiar with. Use the following categories about culture to help you think of questions to ask:

- **Physical aspects** – what people eat, what they wear, what sort of transportation they use, and so forth

- **Customs** – marriage, dating, etc.

- **Celebrations** – holidays, social events

- **Education** – what age children begin school, how formal or informal classes are

B Write a summary of the interview, using the summarizing guidelines listed above.

Pre-writing Tasks
Choose a Topic

A Choose one of the topics below or the topic of your interview in the previous section. You will write a comparison and contrast essay using either the block method or the point-by-point method of writing.

- Wedding customs of two cultures

- Coming-of-age celebrations / rituals in two cultures

B Pair Work Share your topic with a partner. Discuss whether the block method or the point-by-point method would be most suitable for your topic.

Organize Your Ideas

A Complete the chart below with the two or three aspects you are going to write about. Include a brief summary on each aspect from a source (either the interview conducted earlier or an additional source). Indicate the source.

	Topic 1: Culture A ________________	**Topic 1: Culture B** ________________
Aspect 1	Summary: Source:	Summary: Source:
Aspect 2	Summary: Source:	Summary: Source:
Aspect 3	Summary: Source:	Summary: Source:

B Create an outline using either the block or the point-by-point method. See pages 78 and 94 for sample outlines of each method.

Writing Task

Write your comparison and contrast essay. Follow the steps below.

1 Use your chart and outline to decide how many aspects of comparison and contrast to include.

2 Make sure if you use the block method of organization that each paragraph presents all of the points from one side of an issue. If you are going to use the point-by-point method, be sure to include information from both sides for each point in a paragraph.

> **Academic Writing Tip**
>
> **Make Personal Stories More Academic**
>
> In academic writing, personal examples may sometimes be considered too informal. Instead, make the comments more general. Instead of "My family is large" say "Families in the Dominican Republic are generally large."

3 Plan your thesis statement, making sure that it gives the reader a preview of what you will be comparing.

4 Include the following in your essay:

- comparatives and superlatives;
- common expressions of similarity;
- summaries of information and ideas from either written or spoken text;
- acknowledgment of the sources of the summaries;
- at least three of the academic words from the essay in this unit: *adult, adulthood, aid, apparent, area, component, contrast, cultural, culture, define, definition, diverse, element, financial, goal, issue, principle, role, sole, style, traditionally.*

5 After you write your essay, review it and make sure you avoided the mistakes in the Avoid Common Mistakes chart on page 109.

Peer Review

A Exchange your essay with a partner. Answer the following questions as you read your partner's essay, and then share your responses.

1 What is the thesis statement? Underline it.

2 Does the essay use the point-by-point or the block method?

3 Does the writer use any comparative or superlative adjectives?

4 Circle any expressions of similarity that the writer uses.

5 Has the writer included any summaries of information in the essay and cited the sources for them?

6 Is anything confusing? Write a question mark (?) next to it.

7 Provide one compliment (something you found interesting or unusual).

B Use your partner's comments to help you revise your essay. Use the Writer's Checklist on page A2 to review your essay for organization, grammar, and vocabulary.

Comparison and Contrast 4: Adverb Clauses of Contrast and Concession; Transition Words and Phrases That Show Contrast and Concession

Intercultural Communication

1 Grammar in the Real World

You will read an essay about misunderstandings that can happen when people from different cultures attend business meetings together. The essay is an example of one kind of comparison and contrast writing.

A Before You Read What are two cultural differences that might cause misunderstandings in business meetings with people from different cultures? Read the essay. What are assumptions that may cause misunderstandings?

B Comprehension Check Answer the questions.

1 According to the essay, what are three main problems that business people might have when they do business with people from different cultures?

2 Why might the exchange of gifts be inappropriate in some cultures?

3 According to what you have read in this essay, with whom would business people from your culture possibly have misunderstandings? Explain.

C Notice Answer the questions below to help you notice sentences in which two things are contrasted.

1 In the second paragraph, find the words *in contrast* and the word *while* that both signal a contrast. Which one can only come at the beginning of a sentence? Which one is followed by a comma?

2 Find a word on line 37 that signals a contrast. Is it similar to *in contrast* or *while*?

3 Compare the use of the words *even though* and *however* in the fourth paragraph. Which word is similar to *while*? Which one is similar to *in contrast*?

4 Why did the writer use *even though* instead of *while* on lines 44-45?

D Academic Writing Reread the last paragraph of the essay. What three things does the writer do in the conclusion?

INTERNATIONAL Business Etiquette

Large companies want to remain competitive in today's global markets. To reach their goals, they are often required to take their businesses beyond the boundaries of their home countries. Consequently, they need to interact with individuals from other cultures. Cross-cultural business transactions can be challenging since the rules about what is considered appropriate and acceptable and what might be seen as rude vary across cultures. Some aspects of culture are likely to cause misunderstandings in multicultural business situations.

One aspect of culture that may be problematic during business interactions is the perception of time. People in countries such as the United States or Germany commonly pay close attention to schedules and meeting agendas. In those countries, it is impolite if someone habitually arrives late to meetings. In contrast, in countries such as Mexico and Brazil, people tend to see schedules simply as guidelines. They often see deadlines as being more flexible. A Brazilian business person, for example, might find it strange that a U.S. business meeting has an ending time that is nonnegotiable. In Brazil, the length of a meeting is generally dictated by the needs of its participants, while in the United States, a predefined length is often the norm.

The amount of emotion expressed during business interactions can be the cause of other potential cross-cultural problems. This can differ significantly from culture to culture. In some cultures, such as in parts of Italy, people express feelings more openly and argue more passionately about their points of view. For this reason, they may readily show emotion during critical parts of a negotiation, whereas this practice can come across as unprofessional in more emotionally neutral cultures, such as in Sweden. People in these cultures are generally more careful in controlling the feelings they display.

Understanding local customs can also be problematic for business people. Some customs may seem inappropriate in some countries even though they are perfectly acceptable in others. For example, exchanging gifts between the parties involved in a business deal is a common practice in many parts of the world. However, this practice could be seen as inappropriate in other places, such as the United States or Britain. In those cultures, it could even be interpreted as being unethical since gift-giving may be seen as improperly influencing the outcome of the negotiation.

Doing business with people from different cultures can be challenging. When someone is conducting business abroad, it is important not to assume that what is considered polite in one culture is universal. Instead, it is essential to understand and respect other traditions and business practices. Being aware of those differences can give business professionals a competitive edge when conducting business abroad. It might make the difference between a deal's success or failure.

2 Adverb Clauses of Contrast and Concession

Grammar Presentation

Adverb clauses can show many different relationships. Adverb clauses of contrast and concession are common grammatical constructions in academic writing and are especially useful in comparison and contrast writing.

*In some cultures punctuality is important, **while in other cultures**, people arrive at events quite late.*

***Even though most companies train their executives**, cross-cultural problems still arise.*

2.1 Adverb Clauses of Contrast

A Adverb clauses of contrast are used mainly to contrast two things or ideas.

*The official language of Brazil is Portuguese, **while** in Colombia it is Spanish.*

B Adverb clauses of contrast are introduced by the subordinators *while* and *whereas*.

🌐 *While* is much more common than *whereas*. *Whereas* appears in academic writing, but it is rare in spoken English.

*In Mexico, the length of a meeting varies according to the needs of its participants, **while** in the United States, the time is generally set and unchanging.*

*Women in the United States work an average of 41 hours per week, **whereas** women in Europe work about 30 hours per week.*

C An adverb clause of contrast can come before or after the main clause. If it comes first, it is followed by a comma. However, it is more common for an adverb clause of contrast to appear second. Unlike other adverb clauses, a comma can come before an adverb clause of contrast when it appears second to emphasize contrast.

***While** some countries are open to immigration, other countries have strict policies against it.*

*Some customs may be perceived as inappropriate in some countries, **whereas** they are perfectly acceptable in others.*

2.2 Adverb Clauses of Concession

A Adverb clauses of concession express a special kind of contrast. They show that the idea in the main clause is surprising or unexpected.

ADVERB CLAUSE OF CONCESSION
***Although** business people are careful about cultural differences,*

UNEXPECTED INFORMATION
misunderstandings sometimes occur during business transactions.

2.2 Adverb Clauses of Concession (*continued*)

B Adverb clauses of concession are introduced by subordinators: *although, even though, though,* and *while.* A comma can precede an adverb clause of concession to emphasize the contrast.

Note: While can express general contrast as well as concession.

Even though face-to-face communication is preferred, sometimes business has to be conducted virtually.

The company is doing more business with South America, though/while in the past, it conducted business more frequently with Europe.

 # Grammar Application

Exercise 2.1 Adverb Clauses of Contrast

A Listen to an interview about possible differences between business people in the U.S. and Mexico. Check (✓) the correct column for each opinion expressed by Dr. Julio Sanchez.

	In the U.S.	In Mexico
1 Most people are strict about time.	✓	
2 Most people often arrive up to 30 minutes late for business meetings.		
3 It's polite to arrive on time to a dinner party.		
4 Most people share personal information in business meetings.		
5 Most people call each other by their first names as soon as they meet.		
6 Most people have a direct communication style.		
7 Most people may not tell you immediately when they can't attend an event.		

B Use the information from the chart in A and the interview to write sentences using *while* or *whereas.* Sometimes more than one answer is possible.

1 While *most people in Mexico are flexible about time, most people in the United States are very strict.*

2 Whereas ____

3 ____________________________________ , whereas

4 ____________________________________ , while

5 While ____

____

6 ____ , while _______________________

7 Whereas ____

C Pair Work Discuss with a partner your opinions of different behaviors of two cultures that you are familiar with. Write sentences that contrast these behaviors using adverb clauses of contrast, and then report your ideas to the class.

A *In Brazil, people are flexible about time.*

B *In my opinion, it's different in India. There, it's very important to be on time to meetings.*

People are flexible about time in Brazil, while it's very important to be on time in India.

A Combine each pair of sentences about Chinese business culture using the subordinator in parentheses to show relationships of concession. Sometimes more than one answer is possible.

1 a It is not appropriate to treat a Chinese business colleague informally.

   b Doing business in China often involves informal social gatherings where business is not discussed.

(even though) *It is not appropriate to treat a Chinese business colleague informally even though doing business in China often involves social gatherings where business is not discussed.*

2 a Rank is very important.

   b Gender bias is not common.

(though) ____

____

3 a This lack of gesturing does not mean a lack of responsiveness.

   b The Chinese do not gesture or show much body language.

(while) ____

____

4 a It is important to send written information about your company well before your arrival in China.

   b Chinese business people like to meet face-to-face rather than over the phone or by e-mail.

(although) ____

____

5 **a** Chinese business meetings are very formal affairs.

  b The meetings may frequently be interrupted by the ringing of cell phones.

(even though) ____

____

6 **a** Chinese business people are hardworking and serious.

  b Chinese business people have a great sense of humor.

(though) ____

____

7 **a** Some companies may be very successful in their own countries.

  b Their success in China depends on a solid understanding of Chinese culture.

(although) ____

____

B Group Work On a separate sheet of paper, write sentences about the customs of another culture. Use the subordinators of concession in A. Share your sentences with a group. Tell your group members about information that surprised you.

Even though Brazilian people are not very strict about time, it is necessary to schedule an appointment.

Although most business meetings in Morocco are conducted in French, sometimes English is used. Find out which language will be used before your meeting so that you can hire an interpreter if necessary.

3 Transition Words and Phrases That Show Contrast and Concession

Grammar Presentation

Another important way to signal differences or unexpected results in comparison and contrast writing is with transition words and phrases.

*Nodding means yes in some countries; **however**, this is not universal.*

*U.S. executives prefer time limits for meetings. **In contrast**, Greeks see them as less necessary.*

***Despite** their significant cultural differences, Mexico and China are strong trade partners.*

A Use transition words and phrases such as *conversely, however, in contrast, instead, nevertheless, nonetheless, on the contrary,* and *on the other hand* to signal differences.

In some Asian cultures, it is impolite to arrive late at a meeting without an explanation. **In contrast,** *in some European cultures, it is more natural to view schedules and start times as guidelines.*

B Transition words and phrases often begin a sentence and are followed by a comma and an independent clause.

Sometimes they are preceded by a semicolon, but this use is not as common.

People in the United States usually smile when they greet other people. **On the other hand,** *they don't always shake hands.*

Some African cultures do not use the firm handshake common in the United States; **instead,** *they prefer a gentle, slightly longer touching of hands.*

C Transition words and phrases can also come between the subject and the verb. In this case, commas go before and after it.

In some Asian cultures, it is impolite to arrive late at a meeting without an explanation. In some European cultures, **in contrast,** *it is more natural to view schedules and start times as guidelines.*

A *However* is the most common transition word that shows direct contrast. It is similar in meaning to *but.*

In India, gift-giving is common. **However,** *the gifts do not need to be expensive.*

B *On the contrary* rejects the statement that precedes it and then introduces an opposing idea.

Adapting to another culture's customs is not a weakness; **on the contrary,** *it builds stronger relationships and is simply good business.*

C *In contrast* presents two ideas that are different in some way.

Table manners are informal in Canada. **In contrast,** *Moroccan dining usually requires an understanding of a complex set of rules. (These two cultures contrast in their table manners.)*

D *On the other hand* presents contrasting aspects of one idea.

Note: Sometimes in contrast and on the other hand are used interchangeably.

It is not common for people in Turkey to give gifts in a business relationship. **On the other hand,** *they give gifts freely among family members. (Giving gifts in Turkey contrasts in business and personal settings.)*

3.2 Transition Words and Phrases: Differences in Meanings *(continued)*

E *Nevertheless* and *nonetheless* show unexpected facts or ideas.

*Learning about a new culture can be frustrating. **Nevertheless**, a little effort will lead to both personal and professional rewards.*

*Students may be anxious about studying abroad. **Nonetheless**, it is a once-in-a-lifetime chance that should be considered.*

3.3 Prepositions That Show Contrast and Concession

A Prepositions can also signal contrast or concession. Unlike transition words, prepositions are followed by a noun phrase. Often the noun phrase begins with a verb + *-ing*.

Despite and *in spite of* express an unexpected fact or idea.

NOUN PHRASE
Despite/In spite of *their cultural differences, international students usually create close friendships.*

NOUN PHRASE (VERB + *-ING* PHRASE)
Despite/In spite of *coming from different cultures, international students usually become very close friends.*

Instead of replaces one idea or thing with another.

Note: Don't confuse *instead* with *instead of.*

REPLACEMENT IDEA
Some African cultures prefer shaking hands gently

IDEA BEING REPLACED
instead of *shaking hands firmly like in the United States.*

⬚ Grammar Application

Read the email. Complete the sentences about cultural behaviors in different countries. Choose the correct transition words and prepositions.

Dear Professor Jones:

I am in your Anthropology 101 class. I really enjoyed your lecture today. I was not aware of how different other cultures can be. You asked us to e-mail the most interesting things we learned in Chapter 5. The aspects that really caught my attention were:

1   In many countries, shaking the head from side to side is used to indicate *no*. **Nonetheless,/(However,)** in India, individuals move their head from side to side to acknowledge what another person has said.

2   In many places, people greet by shaking hands. **In contrast,/Despite** people hug and kiss in informal circumstances in Latin America.

3   In Japan, the *OK* hand sign does not mean "fine" or "all right" as it does in the United States. **On the other hand,/Instead,** it means "money."

4   It's fairly common knowledge that bowing is a common practice in some Asian countries. **However,/Despite** this knowledge, not many people are aware that the way people bow depends on the social situation and the reason they are bowing.

5   Many businesses spend millions on cross-cultural training. **On the other hand,/Nonetheless,** embarrassing mistakes continue to occur.

6   Many Canadians can be very direct when sharing their opinions. **On the other hand,/In spite of** they can be vague when making social plans.

7   The tendency for many Canadians to be direct is not a sign of unfriendliness. **Nevertheless,/On the contrary,** they are very friendly people.

8   **In spite of/Instead,** the many opportunities for cultural misunderstandings, people continue to conduct business successfully across cultures.

I am looking forward to reading the next chapter.

Thank you,

Maria Yolanda Tavarez

4 Avoid Common Mistakes ⚠ 

1   **Use the correct preposition with *on the other hand*.**

*In the United States, it is appropriate to send a thank-you letter after an interview. ~~In~~ **On** the other hand, a thank-you e-mail is also acceptable in some situations.*
*In some cultures, it is important to ask co-workers about their families. Asking too many personal questions, ~~at~~ **on** the other hand, could seem offensive.*

2   **Use *the other*, not *another* in *on the other hand*.**

*On ~~another~~ **the other** hand, many young American business people speak Chinese.*

3   **Remember to use a comma when transition words and phrases such as *on the contrary* and *in contrast* come at the beginning of a sentence.**

*Business meetings usually begin and end at specific times in the United States. In contrast**,** meeting times in some cultures are not always exact.*

4   **Do not use *but* in sentences with adverb clauses of concession.**

Although many people in the United States speak other languages, ~~but~~ most international business meetings are conducted in English.

Editing Task

Find and correct seven more mistakes in the body paragraph from an essay comparing website differences in different cultures.

     Although the use of corporate websites is universal, ~~but~~ corporate website design is another aspect of doing business that differs from culture to culture. The different website designs for Good Foods are one example. The company operates globally. It wants to appear as though it sells the same quality products everywhere in the world. On another hand, the company wants to appeal to

5   the consumers in each country where it does business. Therefore, the look of its sites differs from country to country. For example, the website for Good Foods in the United States tends to use a limited number of colors. In contrast the company site in India tends to use a great deal of color. The Indian version uses bright colors, such as pink, red, orange, and purple, while the U.S. version of the site uses only shades of blue and gray. This is because the way people interpret colors is

10   cultural. Bright colors suggest "fun" to people in the United States, while blue and gray suggest "importance." In another example, the Good Foods site in Switzerland shows the company's products; however it rarely shows people using or enjoying them. In the other hand, when it does show people, they are usually alone. In contrast the Good Food site for Mexico shows families shopping together and large groups of people enjoying the products. This is because people in

15   Mexico tend to prefer being with others. However people in Switzerland value independence and solitude. Although the main purpose of a company's website is to present important information about the business, but the site must also address the cultural values of the people who view it.

5 Academic Writing

In this section, you will write a comparison and contrast essay using either the point-by-point or the block method. Before you start writing, you will learn how to write effective conclusions.

About Conclusions

The conclusion is the final paragraph of an essay. The conclusion is the writer's last opportunity to make an impact on the reader.

The following are different techniques to end an essay in a way that makes an impact:

1 **Link back to ideas from the first paragraph of the essay.** For example, the writer could link to the "hook" from the introduction or restate the main idea of the essay. In the conclusion below, the writer refers to the hook in the introductory paragraph in which there is an anecdote about a business person who inappropriately arrived "on time" in a culture with which he was unfamiliar.

> *In conclusion, successful international businesses must train their executives to be aware of cultural differences. The business person who arrived "on time" for the social event did not realize how impolite his actions could be. Learning a few key facts about the target culture can lead to greater success in business.*

2 **Ask a thought-provoking question.** The writer can add a question about one of the main points in the essay as a way for readers to continue to think about the topic. However, the writer should not include questions that were not addressed in the essay.

> *In conclusion, successful international businesses must train their executives to be aware of cultural differences. If it is known that there is no universal agreement on what is considered polite, shouldn't people be more willing to respect cultural differences when conducting businesses with other countries?*

3 **Discuss potential consequences.** The conclusion may include a prediction for the future, sometimes by giving a warning, a recommendation, or a call for action.

> *In conclusion, successful international businesses must train their executives to be aware of cross-cultural issues. When someone is doing international business, it is important to never assume that what is considered polite in one culture is universal. Instead, it is essential to understand and respect other traditions.*

4 **Include a relevant quote.** Including a quote from an expert on the essay topic can help create a powerful conclusion. The quote should be closely related to the ideas in the essay.

> *In conclusion, successful international businesses must train their executives to be aware of cultural differences. Of course, knowing individuals is as important as knowing the culture. As Geri-Ann Galanti (2000), a noted professor at UCLA, stated recently, "The danger in considering cultural differences is that of stereotyping people" (p. 335).*

Exercise

A Pair Work Look at the outlines of the following essays. With a partner, discuss ways to write a concluding paragraph for each one.

An Essay Comparing Venezuelan and U.S. Cultures	An Essay Comparing Nelson Mandela and Bill Gates
I Introductory Paragraph **The Hook:** *A description of an American's daily life in Caracas, Venezuela* **Thesis Statement:** *While there are some differences, Venezuela and the United States are similar in several important ways.*	**I Introductory Paragraph** **The Hook:** *"Overcoming poverty is not a task of charity, it is an act of justice," a quote from Nelson Mandela* **Thesis Statement:** *These two influential people of the recent past achieved their goals in very different ways.*
I. Body Paragraph 1: *A comparison and contrast of baseball in Venezuela and the United States*	**II Body Paragraph 1:** *A description of Mandela's contributions to politics, the economy, and fighting poverty*
III Body Paragraph 2: *A comparison and contrast of dating and family life in Venezuela and the United States*	**III Body Paragraph 2:** *A description of Gates's contributions to politics, the economy, and fighting poverty*
IV Conclusion	**IV Conclusion**

B Choose one of the essays outlined above and write a concluding paragraph. Include one of the four techniques for writing an effective conclusion.

Pre-writing Tasks

Choose a Topic

A Choose one of the topics below. You will write a comparison and contrast essay using either the block method or the point-by-point method.

- Three or four aspects of two different cultures, for example, art, music, religion, and family life
- Two important and influential people
- A topic of your own approved by your teacher

B Pair Work Share your topic with a partner. Describe the aspects you are going to compare and contrast. Give each other suggestions about ideas or facts to include.

Organize Your Ideas

Follow the steps below to develop and organize your ideas before you write.

A Complete both outlines below with information for your essay on a separate sheet of paper before you decide which method you will use. There is no "right" choice. The best method depends on what you want to emphasize and how you think your audience will most easily grasp what you are trying to say.

Point-by-Point Method	Block Method
Point 1:	First culture / person:
First culture / person:	Point 1:
Second culture / person:	Point 2:
Point 2:	Point 3:
First culture / person:	Second culture / person:
Second culture / person:	Point 1:
Point 3:	Point 2:
First culture / person:	Point 3:
Second culture / person:	

B Pair Work Look at your outline and your partner's outline, and decide which method will best present the information that you are planning to include in your essays.

Writing Task

Write your comparison and contrast essay. Follow these steps.

1 Write an introduction that includes a hook and a thesis statement.

2 Follow the correct format for either the point-by-point or block method essay pattern.

3 Write your body paragraphs. Do not forget to include topic sentences.

4 Write your conclusion. Use one of the techniques on page 124.

5 Include the following in your essay:

- adverbial clauses of contrast and concession;

- transition words and phrases that show contrast and concession;

- at least three of these academic words from the essay in this unit: *appropriate, aspect, assume, aware, challenging, conduct, consequently, contrast, cultural, culture, display, flexible, global, goal, guideline, inappropriate, individual, interact, interaction, interpret, involved, neutral, norm, outcome, participant, perception, potential, professional, require, schedule, significantly, tradition, unethical, vary.*

6 After you write your essay, review it and make sure you avoided the mistakes in the Avoid Common Mistakes chart on page 123.

Peer Review

A Exchange your essay with a partner. Answer the following questions as you read your partner's essay, and then share your responses.

1 Does the essay have a thesis statement? Underline it.

2 Do the body paragraphs have topic sentences? Underline them.

3 Do the body paragraphs have details that support the topic sentences? Number them.

4 Does the essay use the point-by-point or the block method?

5 How does the writer conclude the essay? What technique did the writer use in the conclusion?

6 Did the writer include transition words of contrast or concession? Circle any that you can find.

7 Is anything confusing? Write a question mark (?) next to it.

8 Provide one compliment (something you found interesting or unusual).

B Use your partner's comments to help you revise your essay. Use the Writer's Checklist on page A2 to review your essay for organization, grammar, and vocabulary.

Narrative 1: Past Perfect; Past Modals; Common Time Clauses

The American Dream

1 Grammar in the Real World

You will read an excerpt from *The Pact: Three Young Men Make a Promise and Fulfill a Dream* (2003), a book about how three men raised in poverty achieved success. The excerpt is an example of narrative writing. Following that you will read a writer's response to the excerpt.

A Before You Read In your opinion, what is the American Dream? Do you believe the American Dream is something that is worth aiming for? Read the essays. According to the writer, are people confident today that they can reach the American Dream? Why or why not?

B Comprehension Check Answer the questions.

1 Why is the story of the three doctors remarkable?

2 What are some events that have negatively impacted or affected the American Dream?

3 According to Rodriguez, why is the American Dream important?

C Notice Follow the instructions below to help you notice how the essay writer shows a sequence of past events.

1 Read the three sentences on lines 46–50 again. Which came first: (a) people had considered the American Dream to be achievable or (b) the idea of the American Dream was damaged? What form of the verb gives you the answer?

2 Reread the sentence on lines 50–53 beginning with "In the late 1980s . . . " Which came first: (a) less job security for Americans or (b) more job security? What form of the verb does the writer use to show this?

D Academic Writing Notice the way writers can add impact to their writing:

1 Underline the shortest sentence in paragraph 1. What impact does the writer create?

2 How does the writer vary the types of sentences in paragraph 2? Circle a simple sentence, and double underline a complex sentence. Underline the three main verbs in lines 21–24.

3 Notice the use of sentences starting with *But* and *And* in paragraph 2. This is generally discouraged in academic writing. What transition words or phrases could replace them?

Excerpt from The Pact: Three Young Men Make a Promise and Fulfill a Dream (2003)

"WE TREAT THEM IN HOSPITALS EVERY DAY. They are young brothers, often drug dealers, gang members, or small-time criminals, who show up shot, stabbed, or beaten after a hustle[1] gone bad.
5 To some of our medical colleagues, they are just nameless thugs,[2] perpetuating crime and death in neighborhoods that have seen far too much of these things. But when we look into their faces, we see ourselves as teenagers, we see our friends, we see what
10 we easily could have become as young adults. And we're reminded of the thin line that separates us – three twenty-nine-year-old doctors (an emergency-room physician, an internist, and a dentist) – from those patients whose lives are filled with danger and desperation.

15 "We grew up in poor, broken homes[3] in New Jersey neighborhoods riddled with crime, drugs, and death, and came of age in the 1980s at the height of a crack epidemic[4] that ravaged communities like ours throughout the nation . . . Two of us landed in
20 juvenile-detention centers[5] before our eighteenth birthdays. But inspired early by caring and imaginative role models, one of us in childhood latched on to[6] a dream of becoming a dentist, steered clear of[7] trouble, and in his senior year of high school persuaded his two
25 best friends to apply to a college program for minority students interested in becoming doctors. We knew we'd never survive if we went after it alone. And so we made a pact:[8] we'd help one another through, no matter what" (Davis, Jenkins, & Hunt, 2003, pp. 1–2).

30 ## Writer's Response
The excerpt from *The Pact: Three Young Men Make a Promise and Fulfill a Dream* might be described as a contemporary version of the American Dream. Simply stated, the American Dream is the belief that if
35 people work hard and play by the rules, they will have a chance to get ahead. The American Dream is based on the belief that people have the same opportunity regardless of their race, creed, color, national origin, gender, or religion.

40 For middle-class Americans, the American Dream typically means that each generation will have more material possessions than the last. For some, achieving the American Dream means having a secure job and owning a home. For others, it is the promise that
45 anyone may rise from poverty to wealth with hard work.

For many years, people had considered the American Dream to be achievable. Several decades ago, things changed. A number of events damaged the idea of the American Dream for the American middle
50 class. In the late 1980s and early 1990s, housing costs increased dramatically, and job security, which had been assured for previous generations, became much less certain. As a result, many people believed that they would be worse off than their parents. Global events
55 such as the Great Recession of 2008 further shook people's confidence about the likelihood of reaching the American Dream. More locally, natural disasters such as Hurricane Maria and Superstorm Sandy significantly affected many people's daily lives and,
60 temporarily at least, shattered their hopes.

For some, it appears that the dream may have died, but does it really matter? *The LA Times* journalist Gregory Rodriguez would say yes. As he states, "The dream is the glue that keeps us all together . . . it's
65 the fabled dream that fuses hundreds of millions of separate, even competing individual dreams into one national collective enterprise" (2010, para. 2). Thus, it is the dream that reassures Americans that the factors for success – ability, strong work ethic, and education – will
70 be rewarded. Like the three doctors who had grown up in such poverty before they achieved success, many people rely on the dream for encouragement as they work hard to create their own versions of the American Dream.

---

[1]**hustle:** the act of tricking people to cheat them out of money

[2]**thug:** a violent person, often a criminal

[3]**broken home:** a family where one parent has left

[4]**crack epidemic:** the widespread drug addiction to crack cocaine in some neighborhoods in the United States during the 1980s

[5]**juvenile-detention center:** a form of prison for young people who are not yet considered adults

[6]**latch on to:** grasp or hold on to

[7]**steer clear of:** avoid

[8]**pact:** an agreement to do something together in the future

2 Past Perfect and Past Perfect Progressive

Grammar Presentation

In academic writing, the past perfect and the past perfect progressive can be used to contrast earlier background events and information with other later events and information in the past.

*By the 1990s, housing costs **had increased** dramatically, and job security **had become** much less certain than for previous generations.*

*When Bob got his first job, his brother **had** already **been working** for several years.*

2.1 Using Past Perfect

A Use the past perfect to describe the first of two completed events in the past. Use the simple past for the later event.

EARLIER EVENT
*By midnight, he **had finished** most of his work,*

LATER EVENT
*so he **decided** to go to bed.*

B You can use the past perfect in sentences with time clauses with *when, by the time,* and *while.* The past perfect is often used in the main clause.

LATER EVENT   EARLIER EVENT
*When she arrived, the class **had** already **started**.*

*By the time she registered for classes, the semester **had** already **begun**.*

The use of the past perfect in sentences with time clauses with *before* and *after* is not necessary since the words indicate a clear time relationship.

*She started college after she **earned**/**had earned** enough money to pay for the first year.*

Note: The use of the simple past in both the main clause and time clause with *when* shows a different time relationship.

FIRST EVENT   SECOND EVENT
When she arrived, the class started.

Choose the past perfect to emphasize that one action was completed before the other.

C Use the past perfect to go back to an earlier time in a narrative or description.

*Nesreen was nervous on her first day of work. She**'d** never **had** a job before.*

D Use the past perfect in narrative writing, and in academic writing in general, to give background reasons and explanations for later past events.

*For years, many people **had considered** the American Dream to be achievable. Then the economy changed.*

2.2 Past Events with Adverbs and Frequency Expressions

Use adverbs of time with the past perfect to emphasize the earlier time period in the past:

after, before, earlier

already, not . . . yet, still . . . not

ever, just, never, recently

*No one in her family **had** ever **attended** college before.*

*She**'d** already **talked** to a few colleges, but she **hadn't applied** yet. She needed to find a way to pay the tuition.*

*They**'d** recently **applied** for a grant and were waiting for a final response.*

2.3 Using Past Perfect and Past Perfect Progressive

A Like the past perfect, the past perfect progressive can give background reasons or describe past events.

Note: As with other progressive forms, don't use past perfect progressive with stative verbs, such as *be*, *know*, and *seem*.

PAST PERFECT

*They **had experienced** many challenges, so they **decided** to make a pact.*

PAST PERFECT PROGRESSIVE

*They **had been experiencing** many challenges, so they **decided** to make a pact.*

*She **had known** that she wanted to be in education since she was a young girl.*

NOT

She ~~had been knowing~~ that she wanted to be in education since she was a young girl.

B Use the past perfect progressive to emphasize an ongoing past action leading up to a point in the past.

This action may have been occurring when another past action took place.

🌐 The past perfect progressive form is much less common than the past perfect.

*He**'d been talking about** applying to medical school for a long time. Finally, last January, he applied.*

FIRST EVENT

*They**'d been working** for about an hour*

SECOND EVENT

when the bell rang.

🖥 Grammar Application

Exercise 2.1 Simple Past and Past Perfect

A Complete the sentences about an immigrant who came to the United States. Use the simple past or past perfect form of the verbs in parentheses.

1 Naresh ___*had studied*___ (study) English for three years in his native country, India, before he ___*came*___ (come) to the United States.

2 Naresh ___________________ (arrive) in the United States six months ago to study.
He ___________________ (never/be) here before.

3 At first, he ___________________ (stay) in a motel because
   he ___________________ (neglect) to look for a place to live
   before arriving.

4 Naresh's parents ___________________ (be) worried about
   him because after a month, he still ___________________
   (not find) an apartment.

5 They ___________________ (contact) their friend Sam
   who was living in the United States. Naresh's parents
   ___________________ (help) Sam 25 years earlier to adjust
   to living in India.

6 Sam and his wife, Lea, ___________________ (be) good
   friends with Naresh's parents. They ___________________
   (go) to visit Naresh's family several times.

7 Naresh ___________________ (hope) to live on his own, but after struggling so much, he
   ___________________ (be) happy to accept Sam and Lea's offer to stay with them.

8 Sam and Lea ___________________ (give) Naresh as much help as they could, just like
   Naresh's parents ___________________ (assist) Sam 25 years earlier.

B Pair Work Explain your answers in A to a partner. Do you agree?

*First, Naresh studied English and second, he came to the United States. So we
need to use the past perfect form* had studied *and the simple past form* came.

Exercise 2.2 Past Perfect and Past Perfect Progressive

A Complete the sentences about a South Korean woman who moved to the United States.
Circle the past perfect or past perfect progressive form of the verbs. For some items, both
forms are possible.

1 Mi Young's mother **had planned /(had been planning)** to visit her daughter in the
   United States for several years, but by Mi Young's fifth year in New York, her mother still
   (hadn't visited)/ hadn't been visiting her.

2 Mi Young's mother **had gone / had been going** to Los Angeles once before to visit her
   sister when she was much younger, and she **had wanted / had been wanting** to return
   ever since then.

3 At one point, it seemed as if Mi Young might come home because she **had lost / had been
   losing** her job and she **had looked / had been looking** for a new job for several months.

4 Mi Young **had thought / had been thinking** about moving back to South Korea when she
   got a job offer in Los Angeles. It was a company that a friend of hers **had just started / had
   been starting** to work for.

5 Mi Young's mom **had worried / had been worrying** about traveling all the way to New York,
   so she was happy when Mi Young moved to Los Angeles. The flight was a lot shorter!

6 Also, her mother **had had / had been having** a nice time in Los Angeles on her first trip,
   so she **had hoped / had been hoping** since then that Mi Young might get a job there.

B Pair Work Think of a major change in your life or in the life of someone you know, such as a move, a marriage, or a new job. Describe the events leading up to the change. Use the past perfect and the past perfect progressive where necessary.

My boyfriend and I had been talking about getting married for over a year when he proposed to me. We'd been together for three years by that time. I'd known soon after we met that I was going to marry him, but I was still nervous about making the commitment. When I told my parents, they weren't surprised at all, but they thought I was too young. I was 21 at the time . . .

3 Past Modals and Modal-like Expressions

Grammar Presentation

Past modals and modal-like expressions are used to give a perspective on events (whether the speaker or writer saw the event as possible, necessary, desirable, and so on).	I **should have studied** French when I was in high school. Joanna **could not finish** college in four years because she **had to** work full-time.

3.1 Past Modals and Modal-like Expressions

A Use these modal-like expressions for past necessity and lack of necessity:

had to to say something was necessary in the past

did not have to to say something wasn't necessary in the past

*The three friends came from poor families, so they **had to** find a way to pay for their education.*

*They **did not have to** pay for their college education because they got scholarships.*

B Use these modals for past permission and prohibition:

could to say something was allowed or permitted in the past

could not to say something was not allowed or permitted in the past

*In the past, minority students **could apply** for special college grants.*

*Nonminority students **could not apply** for these special college grants.*

C Use these modals for disapproval or regret over an action taken or not taken:

should have, should not have, and *could have*

*I **should have applied** for a work study job. (But I didn't, and I regret it.)*

*She **shouldn't have missed** so many classes. (But she did and now she's failing.)*

*We **could have asked** for help. (But we didn't and now we're sorry.)*

D Use these modals for possibility or impossibility of a past action:

could / might have to show possibility

He *could / might have found out* about the job opening through the school's career center. (It's possible because I know he went there.)

could not have to show impossibility

We *could not have predicted* that the number of college applications would increase so much this year. (It was impossible to predict.)

3.2 *Would* and *Used To* for Past Habits

A Use *would / used to* + base form of the verb to describe habits or routines that happened regularly in the past, but don't happen now.

With *would*, a past time reference – such as a past time clause – must be used or understood.

Would is more common than *used to* in academic writing.

While I was living in my country, I *would go* for long walks.

I *used to study* on the bus to school every day. Now I drive my car to school, so I can't study then.

B Use *used to* with stative verbs (verbs like *have* or *be*) that describe states or conditions in the past. Do not use *would* to describe states or conditions in the past.

I *used to be* a manager at a hotel, but now I work at a bank.

My brother *used to have* a bike. Now he has a car.

I *used to like* long walks in the country.

NOT I ~~would~~ like long walks in the country.

3.3 *Was / Were + Supposed To* and *Was / Were Going To* for Past Expectation

Use *was / were + supposed to* and *be going to* + base form of the verb to describe required or planned actions in the past that did not take place.

They are often followed by *but* and a clause that explains why the action was not completed.

The foundation *was supposed to provide* full funding for 30 students.

The students *were going to get* part-time jobs, *but there were none available*.

She *was supposed to start* classes this fall, *but she didn't have enough money for tuition*.

Grammar Application

Complete the sentences about a woman who found success because of her hard work. Use the verbs in parentheses and a modal *(could, could have, had to, might have, should have)*. Use the cues at the beginning of the sentences to decide on the appropriate modal.

1 [necessary] Sarah ___*had to work*___ (work) when she was young because her father's salary wasn't enough for the family.

2 [not necessary] Every day, Sarah went to school and then went to work at a pizza shop. Her school and the pizza shop were close to home, so she _______________ (drive) or take the bus.

3 [possible] When Sarah finished high school, she wanted to go to college, but she didn't have enough money. She _______________ (win) a scholarship because she had high grades, but she never applied for one.

4 [regret] Later she realized that she _______________ (apply) for every possible scholarship.

5 [not necessary] Sarah decided that she could be a success even without a college education. Because she _______________ (go) to school anymore, she began working full time.

6 [possible] She worked 60 hours a week at the pizza shop and made a lot of money, yet she hardly spent any. Her thriftiness _______________ (be) the result of growing up in a poor household.

7 [not permitted] After a few years, the owner of the pizza shop decided he wanted to sell the shop. Sarah wanted to buy it. She didn't have enough money, so she tried to take out a loan at the bank, but she _______________ (get) a loan.

8 [allowed] The pizza shop owner really liked Sarah because she was such a hard worker. He told her that she _______________ (buy) the shop from him and pay him over five years.

9 [disapproval] The owner's friends thought it was a bad idea. They told him he _______________ (loan) her the money, but he knew he had made the right decision.

10 [possibility] Once Sarah had bought the shop, she made it more successful than it had ever been. No one _______________ (predict) how successful Sarah would be.

11 [impossibility] Sarah continued to work hard, and after 10 years, she bought five more shops. She herself _______________ (guess) that she would one day become such a successful businesswoman.

A Listen to the story about Rita and Edwin, a couple from the Dominican Republic. Write *T* if the statement is true or *F* if the statement is false.

1. _*F*_ Rita and Edwin used to live in New York.

2. _____ Every semester, they would enroll in the free English classes offered at schools.

3. _____ In his English classes, Edwin would always sit next to Spanish-speaking students.

4. _____ When she started classes, Rita wouldn't speak when the teacher called on her.

5. _____ She used to always start crying when she got nervous in class.

6. _____ Rita would often talk to her classmates.

7. _____ When he got a job at a hotel, Edwin would take a bus to get there.

8. _____ Rita and Edwin used to dream of a better life.

B Pair Work Tell your partner about your past habits, and contrast them with your current life. Explain to your partner why your past habits have changed.

I used to work as a waiter in a restaurant, but now I'm a full-time student.
I realized that it was difficult to work and study at the same time, so I quit my job.

A The chart below shows expectations and plans that John and people who knew him had about his life and the reasons why the plans did not come true. Write sentences about John using the information in the chart and *was/were supposed to* and *was/were going to*.

Expectations	Reasons Why the Plans Did Not Come True
1 Everyone expected John to become a doctor.	Nobody knew that he couldn't stand the sight of blood.
2 John planned to major in biology.	He changed his mind and decided to major in business instead.
3 John and his friends planned to go into business together after college.	They didn't have enough money.
4 John planned to move to California to find a job.	He was offered a job in Japan.
5 Everyone thought John would marry his high school sweetheart.	He fell in love with a girl in Japan.
6 John's parents planned to visit him this month.	His father broke his leg, so they postponed the trip.

1 *John was going to be a doctor, but nobody knew he couldn't stand the sight of blood.*

2 ____

3 ____

4 ____

5 ____

6 ____

B Pair Work Tell your partner about plans that you and others had that changed. Explain why they changed. Then tell your partner about plans that people you know had that changed and why they changed.

I was going to major in computer science, but I decided I was more interested in history. My brother has always loved animals. We always thought he was going to be a veterinarian, but he ended up majoring in business. He said that he changed his mind when he started working at a bank. He really wants to own his own business some day.

4 Common Time Clauses 🌐

Vocabulary Presentation

Time clauses show time or sequence. It is common to use these constructions in longer, more complex sentences in a narrative.	*After I finished high school, I had to find a job.* *I started practicing interview skills when I heard that I had a job interview.*

4.1 Common Time Clauses

A Dependent clauses that show a time relationship begin with subordinators such as *after*, *as*, *before*, and *while*. They are sometimes called adverb clauses of time.	*Life in the U.S. was difficult at first. I did my English homework while my baby was sleeping.*

B Use these subordinators to show different aspects of time and sequence:

after to show that the event in the time clause happened first

> FIRST   SECOND
> *After he started working on campus, it was very difficult to keep up with his classes.*

before to show that the event in the time clause happened second

> SECOND   FIRST
> *Before I moved to this country, I did not know how to cook.*

every time to show repeated events that are connected in either the past or present

> *Every time they moved, the children had to adjust to a new school.*

since (often using the present perfect or past perfect in the main clause) to show when an action or state started in the past

> *He's been working since he left high school.*

once, when, and *as soon as* to show that one event quickly followed another event

> *Once I finished college, I started looking for a job.*

when, while, and *as* to show that both events happened at the same time

> *He worked full-time at a grocery store while he was going to college.*

until to show a time frame that continues up to a certain time or event

> *I had to work night shifts until I found a better job.*

🌐 *Before, when, until,* and *after* are the most frequently used subordinating conjunctions in academic writing.

Vocabulary Application

Exercise 4.1 Common Time Clauses

Combine the sentences about the author Stephen King using the subordinator in parentheses.

1 Stephen King struggled a lot in his life. Then he became a famous author.

   (before) *Stephen King struggled a lot in life before he became a famous author.*

2 He was two years old. His father left.

   (when) _______________________________________

3 His father left. Then his mother struggled to take care of him and his brother.

   (after) _______________________________________

4 He was 12. He became interested in writing horror stories.

(when) ____

5 He was in school. He wrote many stories.

(while) ____

6 He sold stories to his classmates. Then the teachers asked him to stop.

(until)____

7 His first short story was published. Then he graduated college.

(before)____

8 His mother died. Then his first novel, *Carrie*, was published.

(after)____

Exercise 4.2 More Common Time Clauses

A Complete the paragraph about the life of Dr. Martin Luther King, Jr. Circle the correct subordinators using information from the time line of events in his life.

1955 – Rosa Parks arrested on December 1 for refusing to give up her seat on a bus to a white passenger in Montgomery, Alabama; started a boycott on December 5 to stop segregation on Montgomery buses
1956 – In June, segregation law declared unconstitutional; in December, bus segregation stopped
1963 – King delivered "I Have a Dream" speech at the Lincoln Memorial in Washington, D.C.
1968 – King assassinated at the Lorraine Motel in Memphis, Tennessee
1986 – Birthday of Dr. Martin Luther King, Jr. declared a national holiday
2011 – Memorial statue of King put up in Washington, D.C.

August, 1963, at the March on Washington

Dr. Martin Luther King, Jr. was an influential leader in the 1950s and 1960s in the Civil Rights movement, a movement that ended segregation and discrimination of African Americans in American society. **After / While** other leaders were considering violence as the way to bring about social
(1)
changes in the early 1950s, King was urging people to use nonviolent means, such as boycotts and demonstrations. The movement did not become energized **until / as soon as** Rosa Parks, a social
(2)
activist, refused to give her seat on a bus to a white man. On December 1, 1955, black residents in Montgomery, Alabama, boycotted the buses and elected King as their leader. **Once / As** the boycott
(3)
continued into 1956, King's reputation as a courageous leader grew, and his outstanding speaking skills inspired many to join the movement. **Before / After** the U.S. Supreme Court declared Alabama's
(4)

segregation laws unconstitutional in June, segregation on Montgomery buses finally ended that following December. **Once / Since** the Supreme (5) Court made its decision, King ended the boycott. In 1963, King delivered his famous "I Have a Dream" speech. Just five years **since / after** he (6) delivered that speech, King was assassinated in Memphis, Tennessee. **Since / Until** the Civil Rights Act of 1964 was passed, many people have (7) benefited from it. Among other provisions, the act made it illegal to discriminate against someone based on race, religion, and gender. Dr. Martin Luther King, Jr. continues to be an icon for the civil rights movement. **As / Until** more and more people recognized King's significant (8) contribution to civil rights and equality over time, political figures began to ask for a day of remembrance. The first Martin Luther King Day of Service was observed in 1986. In 2011, a memorial was dedicated to King on the National Mall in Washington, D.C.

B Make a time line similar to the one in A with important events in your life or the life of someone that you admire on a separate piece of paper. Explain the events on your time line to a partner. Use time clauses.

Since I was young, I've wanted to go to college to study math. Before I started college, I spent two years in the army. As soon as I got out of the army, I sent out applications for college.

5 Avoid Common Mistakes ⚠ 

1 **Remember to use the past participle after *had* when forming the past perfect.**

       gone
He had ~~went~~ to college, so he already had a degree.

          come
Blanca's family had ~~came~~ to the United States when she was still a child.

2 **Remember to use the past perfect progressive, not the past progressive, in the main clause for an action that happens in an earlier time frame than the action in the *when* clause.**

      had been taking
She ~~was taking~~ care of children for many years when she realized she needed an A.A. degree.

       had been working
Ahmet ~~was working~~ in a restaurant for a long time when he decided to go to college.

3 **Remember to use the simple past, not the past perfect, for a single completed action or state. The past perfect is often used to describe a previous time before another past time.**

      graduated
I ~~had graduated~~ from college last year.

Editing Task

Find and correct nine more mistakes in the use of the past perfect and past perfect progressive in the narrative paragraphs on changing careers.

Changing Careers

Jessica had always loved photography, even as a child. She *had been asking* ~~was asking~~ for a camera for a long time when her father had gave her one on her tenth birthday. She would take her camera everywhere and record the small moments of everyday life that caught her eye: a cluster of leaves on the sidewalk, or a spider web on a garden fence. Jessica had always see photography as a hobby. Moreover, since she had

5 came from a family that had endured economic hardships when she was growing up, she had always know that she had to choose a career that paid well and was secure. Therefore, after high school, she got a degree in landscape design. She was considering a job with the city during her last year of college, but when her uncle, the owner of a landscape company, asked her to work for him, she changed her mind. She had joined his landscaping business right after graduation. However, Jessica never lost her love

10 of photography. She eventually bought herself a higher quality camera and continued to take pictures whenever she had the opportunity.

Jessica was working at the landscaping company for about two years when her uncle decided to build a website to advertise the business. He needed images of the company's best work to publish on the site and immediately thought of Jessica. She was taking photos of the company's projects the entire time that

15 she had worked there. The website had been a success. More importantly, other companies saw it and wanted to know who the great photographer was. Soon, Jessica was working full time as a photographer. Her uncle missed Jessica's presence, but everyone was pleased that she was now earning a living doing something that she truly loved.

6 Academic Writing

In this section, you will write an introductory paragraph for an essay. This paragraph will contain a narrative. Before you start writing, you will learn how to use a range of sentence structures in narrative writing to add impact to your writing.

About Sentence Variety

There are several ways to add impact to your writing, such as by using precise vocabulary and by including clear and convincing examples. Another way is by using a variety of sentence structures:

1 **Alternate short and long sentences.** While academic writers often use compound and complex sentences, short sentences are an effective way to emphasize important information. In a narrative, a short sentence may contain the climax or the turning point of the story.

> *When William Jefferson Blythe III was born in 1946, his father had died in a car crash three months earlier. Billy, as he was known as a child, was a good student and loved to play the saxophone. While he excelled in school, Billy's family life was troubled. His stepfather, a man named Roger Clinton, was an abusive alcoholic who was difficult to live with. As a teenager, Billy took his stepfather's name and continued to protect his mother and younger brother from his stepfather's drunken rage whenever he could. This boy certainly did not have an easy time in his early life, but it did not stop him from going on to do great things. In fact, in 1992 he achieved what very few people have ever done. Bill Clinton was elected president of the United States.*

2 **Use a variety of words and phrases and vary their position in the sentence.** Do not always start sentences the same way. Find different ways to connect ideas between sentences. Use a variety of connectors.

Original	Variety of Words and Phrases
The American Dream consists of many factors. For example, it includes personal wealth and job satisfaction. When one considers personal wealth, it is measured in many ways. For example, wealth can be measured in salary, property, and investments. Job satisfaction is complex. For example, some people measure it by how happy a person is while doing the job, while other people measure it by how important or relevant the work is.	*The American Dream consists of many factors such as personal wealth and job satisfaction. When one considers personal wealth, it is measured in many ways, including salary, property, and investments. Job satisfaction is complex. Some people, for example, measure it by how happy a person is while doing the job, while other people measure it by how important or relevant the work is.*

3 **Place key ideas in the main clause of a sentence.** It is usually a good idea to put the most important idea in the main clause of a sentence. In addition, it adds more impact to put that clause at the end of the sentence, especially if you are going to write more about that idea in the next sentence.

Two Ideas:	Emphasizing Idea 1	Emphasizing Idea 2
Idea 1: Many people know what the American Dream means to them. **Idea 2**: Few people can clearly define the American Dream.	*While few people can clearly define it, **many people know what the American Dream means to them**.*	*Although many people know what the American Dream means to them, **few people can clearly define it**.*

4 **Avoid using too many words to explain an idea.** The more concise, the better.

Wordy: *Maria thought, but was not really sure, that life in the United States would be better for her than the life she had in her country.*

Better: *Maria assumed that life in the United States would be better than life in her country.*

Exercise

A **Read the paragraph below. Then rewrite the sentences as indicated to improve the writing and give it more impact.**

(1) The night before my first job interview, I was so nervous I could not sleep. (2) Having eaten a large supper earlier as well as being nervous, it wasn't surprising that with my full stomach and nerves that I found myself having a great deal of trouble when I tried to fall asleep. (3) When I finally fell asleep, my alarm clock turned off as a result of a power outage. (4) The next morning, as a result of oversleeping, I had to move very fast to get to the interview on time. (5) I arrived at the interview very hungry since I hadn't had time to eat breakfast. (6) During the interview, the manager offered me a piece of candy. (7) I ate it and, after a few moments, I felt something strange in my mouth. (8) I realized that a filling in my tooth had come out! (9) I ran from the office covering my mouth, and I learned that I should never eat anything at a job interview.

1 Make sentence 2 more concise and write it below.

____

____

2 Sentences 3 and 4 contain the same connector. Replace one with a different connector.

____

____

3 Change the order of ideas in sentence 5 so that it ends with the idea of arriving hungry.

____

____

4 Revise sentence 9 so that it is three sentences. Make the last sentence the shortest.

____

____

B Pair Work Compare your revised sentences with a partner's. Did you make the same changes? Read your sentences aloud. Whose sentences make more of an impact?

Pre-writing Tasks

Choose a Topic

A Choose one of the topics below. You will write one paragraph that contains a narrative to illustrate your topic.

- A narrative about job hunting that illustrates the topic sentence: *Job candidates need to be well-prepared for anything during the interview process.*

- A narrative about interviewing that illustrates the topic sentence: *Every interview shows something important about the interview process.*

- A narrative about a trait that is considered to be necessary to be an excellent student or employee and that illustrates the topic sentence: *One important trait that many students/employees display is ___________________ .*

B Pair Work Share your chosen topic with a partner. Provide suggestions about ideas or facts to include. Make a list.

Organize Your Ideas

A Write down as many events and details for your story as you can. This is a brainstorm, so don't worry about the order of the events. Just write down words and phrases that remind you of the story.

B Pair Work Share your brainstorm with a partner and together choose which events and details should be included in the story. Write out the events that you chose to include in the order that they happened. Use these notes to help you write the story.

Writing Task

Write your narrative paragraph. Follow the steps below.

1 Review your notes.

2 Write your narrative. Remember to include a topic sentence.

3 Include the following in your paragraph:

- the past perfect and past perfect progressive;
- past modals and modal-like expressions;
- common time clauses;
- a variety of sentence lengths and structures to add impact;
- at least three of these academic words from the essay in this unit: *achieve, adult, assure, colleague, contemporary, create, decade, dramatically, ethic, factor, gender, generation, job, medical, minority, previous, rely, secure, security, survive, version.*

Academic Writing Tip

Avoid the Simple Present in Narratives

Use past forms of verbs rather than the present forms to describe events in narratives. The use of the simple present is often considered more informal.

4 After you write your paragraph, review it and make sure you avoided the mistakes in the Avoid Common Mistakes chart on page 140.

Peer Review

A Exchange your paragraph with a partner. Answer the following questions as you read your partner's story, and then share your responses.

1 Does the writer's story illustrate the topic sentence well?

2 Did the writer include any verbs in the past perfect tense when contrasting two events in the past to show that one occurred before the other? Circle any verbs in the past perfect tense.

3 Did the writer appropriately include any past modals?

4 Are there any time clauses? Do they help make the order of events in the narrative clear?

5 Which is the shortest sentence in the narrative? Underline it. Does this sentence deserve to receive the emphasis it does?

6 Are there any overly long sentences? How could they be improved?

7 Is anything confusing? Write a question mark (?) next to it.

8 Provide one compliment (something you found interesting or unusual).

B Use your partner's comments to help you revise your paragraph. Use the Writer's Checklist on page A2 to review your paragraph for organization, grammar, and vocabulary.

Narrative 2: Demonstratives; Common Time Signals

Immigration

1 Grammar in the Real World

You will read an essay about the history of immigration in the United States. The essay is an example of a historical narrative.

A Before You Read Why do people immigrate to the United States? What are some of the problems that immigrants encounter? Read the essay. How has the United States benefited from immigration throughout the years?

B Comprehension Check Answer the questions.

1 Describe the immigrants who traveled to the United States in the seventeenth century.

2 When and why did the U.S. government start to restrict entrance into the United States?

3 Why does the writer say that the United States will continue to be built with the help of immigrants?

C Notice Follow the instructions below to help you understand the use of demonstratives and time words to define different periods of time.

1 On lines 20–23, notice the use of the word *these* in the sentence "Even though some of these immigrants . . .". What does *these* refer to?

2 On lines 27–28, notice the use of *that* in "During that period . . .". What does *that* refer to?

3 In the second paragraph, underline the words the writer uses to define two different periods of time.

D Academic Writing Work with a partner and answer the questions:

1 Who do you think is the audience (main readers) of this essay?

2 What is the purpose of this essay?

Immigration
and the United States

SINCE THE SEVENTEENTH CENTURY, immigrants from all over the world have come to the United States in search of safety, freedom, and economic opportunities. Immigration patterns have varied over time, with distinct periods of immigration from different countries. In each of these periods, immigrants helped shape U.S. society and the economy. However, the flow of immigrants has also brought challenges that continue into the present.

The period from the seventeenth century through the early nineteenth century is the first and longest U.S. immigration wave. During this time, most immigrants came from Europe, including France and the Netherlands. The number of immigrants was small, and most of the newcomers became farmers. By the 1820s, this pattern started to change. From the 1820s to 1880s, approximately 15 million immigrants settled in the United States (Diner, 2008). Even though some of these immigrants decided to work in agriculture in the Midwest and Northeast, many more moved to big cities, such as New York City and Boston.

The immigration wave that took place between the 1890s and the beginning of the twentieth century is often referred to as the flood of immigrants. During that period, nearly 25 million immigrants arrived in the United States (Diner, 2008). They were mainly young Europeans from countries such as Italy, Greece, Hungary, and Poland.

Each group of immigrants presented distinct characteristics. Some groups were less formally educated and some were mostly young, for example. However, they all contributed to the growth of many industries, including steel, automobile, and textile. Because of them, the United States turned into one of the world's most powerful countries.

Over the course of the late nineteenth and early twentieth centuries, protests over immigrants grew. Many people were troubled by the new religions and customs that immigrants brought to the United States. As a result, in 1921 the government passed laws limiting the number of immigrants allowed to enter each year. Even though immigrants contributed to the economic growth of the United States, the country made it difficult for them to enter.

In the early 2000s, the immigration debate was reignited due to high numbers of immigrants, documented and undocumented. Opponents argued that immigrants took jobs away from people and that the cost of maintaining their welfare was a drain on the education and health care systems (Diner, 2008). Although the arguments continue to this day, it is important to remember that the country was and will continue to be built with the help of immigrants.

2 Demonstratives

Grammar Presentation

| Demonstratives (*this*, *that*, *these*, *those*) are used in all kinds of writing to connect ideas or give coherence. | *In my neighborhood, there are people from all over the world. Most of **these** people have good jobs.*

*The article is about recent immigration. **That** topic always generates interesting conversation.* |

2.1 Demonstratives

| Use demonstratives (*this*, *that*, *these*, *those*) to show physical distance from the speaker or distance in time.

Use *this/these* to refer to people or things close in time and space to the speaker.

Use *that/those* to refer to people or things in a more distant time and space. | ***This** unit is about immigration. Let's look at the first page.*

*I remember **those** days when I'd been in this new country for only three weeks and didn't speak any English.* |

2.2 Demonstratives That Connect Ideas

A Use demonstratives to connect ideas that are close to each other and to make the text cohesive. These are also called demonstrative adjectives.	*Immigrants came from all over Europe. Most of **these** immigrants opted for farming. (**These** immigrants refers to the immigrants from all over Europe.)* *The flood of immigrants occurred between the 1890s and the beginning of the twentieth century. During **that** period, nearly 25 million immigrants arrived in the United States.*
B You can use demonstratives without a noun. When they stand alone, they are pronouns. You can also use *it* for the same purpose.	*Climate change affects everyone. Indeed, **this** is the most important environmental issue of our time. (**This** refers to climate change.)* *Climate change affects everyone. Indeed, **it** is the most important environmental issue of our time. (**It** refers to climate change.)*
C Use demonstrative pronouns to summarize or refer to a previously mentioned idea in the same paragraph.	*Economic disparity is widespread and increasing. **This** is an especially significant problem for developing countries.* *(**This** refers to the fact that economic disparity is increasing.)*

2.2 Demonstratives That Connect Ideas *(continued)*

D Use a demonstrative with a noun that summarizes or clarifies what it refers to, for example:

approach, aspect, development, experience, factor, reason, phenomenon, topic

Nearly 25 million Europeans traveled to the United States at the end of the nineteenth century and early twentieth century. *That development* changed the demographics of the country. (*That development* refers to the idea of the previous sentence.)

E The summary word or phrase that follows demonstratives can reflect the writer's opinion about a previously described topic, for example:

controversial argument, indisputable fact, questionable claim, undisputed fact

Some people believe immigration leads to increases in crime. *This controversial argument* has been challenged by many.

Millions of people have immigrated to the United States. *This undisputed fact* constitutes one of the central elements in the country's development.

Grammar Application

Exercise 2.1 Demonstratives

A Read the sentences about immigration in Europe. Complete the sentences with the correct demonstratives. Sometimes more than one answer is possible.

1 The European Union has expanded in recent years to include over two dozen countries. ___*This*___ has contributed to increased immigration all over Europe.

2 In 2004, ten countries joined the European Union. _______________ countries included Hungary, Poland, Lithuania, and Slovakia.

3 Citizens of European Union member nations have permission to live in any EU country where they work. _______________ makes it fairly easy for people to move from one EU country to another.

4 About 4.7 million people immigrated to one of the EU Member States in 2015 alone. _______________ figure includes not only people from outside the EU but also people moving between EU countries.

5 There are about five million immigrants living in Italy. _______________ people make up just over 8 percent of the population.

6 In 2017, 25,600 people wanted to immigrate to Sweden for asylum.[1] _______________ was 11.72 percent less than in 2016.

[1] **asylum:** protection or safety

B Pair Work Take turns with a partner explaining what each demonstrative refers to in the sentences.

In sentence 1, This refers to the expansion of the European Union.

A Choose the correct word or words to complete the paragraphs that explain one writer's view of the challenges of immigration.

Millions of people move to new countries every year. This **phenomenon**/reason
(1)
can cause challenges for both the residents of the host country and for the immigrants. Often, the people from the host country and the immigrants have difficulty relating to each other and understanding each other's customs. Also, the language of the host country and the immigrants' language are sometimes very different. If people cannot speak to each other, they cannot begin to understand each other. This **fact**/**argument** may be
(2)
the underlying cause of most misunderstandings between residents and immigrant groups. People often fear what they do not understand.

However, people disagree about which language immigrants should speak. This **development**/**controversial issue** can produce very different responses. Some people
(3)
believe that immigrants should stop speaking their native language and speak the host country's language, even in their homes. They feel that immigrants will be able to assimilate better if they adopt the host country's language. This **questionable claim**/**aspect** is directly
(4)
opposed to the opinion of those who believe that it is important for immigrants to continue to speak their own language while they learn the host country's language. Many believe that this second **aspect**/**approach** is the best one for young children. These **people**/**factors**
(5)   (6)
argue that individuals who have a strong command of their own language are better able to learn a new language. This **argument**/**topic** seems to have some validity since research
(7)
shows that immigrant children who cannot read and write in their parent's language have trouble learning to read and write their adopted country's language.

B Pair Work Discuss your answers in A with a partner. What do you think the writer's opinion is about immigrants and language? How do you know? Do you agree or disagree with the writer's opinion? Write a response of four to five sentences to the writer's opinions using demonstratives and the words in A. Present it to another pair or to the class.

The writer believes that immigration can cause problems for countries and immigrants. We understand that there are sometimes issues that need to be resolved, but we strongly feel that this phenomenon is actually, in the long run, good for both the countries and the immigrants because . . .

3 Common Time Signals 🌐

Vocabulary Presentation

Time signals are important to use in narrative writing to make the sequence of events or ideas easier to follow.

Over the past twenty years, immigration has become a controversial issue in many European countries.

This is not **the first time** in U.S. history that immigrants have been criticized.

3.1 Common Time Signals

A The most common time signals are prepositional phrases such as:

by + specific time

The immigration situation changed **by** the mid 1800s.

from + specific time + *through / to* + specific time

The first and longest immigration era stretched **from** the seventeenth century **to** the early nineteenth century.

after / since + specific time

After the end of World War I (from 1914 to 1918), Congress changed the nation's basic policy about immigration.

over / during the course of + specific time

Over the course of the late nineteenth and early twentieth centuries, the government took measures to slow down immigration.

over the past / next / last + time period

Over the last / past 20 years, immigration has increased.

in the past / next / last + time period

In the next 10 years, immigration is likely to decrease.

for + time period

The high rate of immigration continued **for** almost one hundred years.

B Time adverbs are also considered time signals:

already, always, ever, just, lately, never, now, recently, since, yet, the first / last time.

We've **always** lived in this neighborhood.

I will **never** again feel so helpless.

I **now** work in a clinic that serves immigrants.

It felt great **the first time** I realized I could make my own choice.

The debate over immigration has heated up **recently**.

Note: Use the present perfect with the expression *this is the first time.*

INCORRECT: **This is the first time** I ~~read / am reading~~ about immigration issues.

CORRECT: **This is the first time** I've read about immigration issues.

C Use *every day*, *once* (*once more / once again / once or twice*), and *twice* to indicate frequency.

Every day, I'm amazed by how far I've gone.

By 2000, the United States had **once again** become a nation of immigrants.

D Use *time* + *later / earlier* to indicate when something happened in relation to another event.

I left my neighborhood when I was just 11. <u>Years</u> **later**, I returned to Boston to go to medical school.

Vocabulary Application

You will listen to an essay written by a Vietnamese immigrant to the United States. Listen and write the missing words. Then listen and check your answers.

I was born in Vietnam. My family moved to the United States <u>**when I was eight**</u>.
(1)
_______________________, I lived in San Jose,
(2)
California. All our neighbors were immigrants.

_______________________ a new immigrant family
(3)
arrived, we helped them settle. We lived there

_______________________.
(4)

_______________________, I studied very hard
(5)
in school. My parents taught me to value education
even though they were poorly educated. Then

_______________________, I went to college and
(6)
_______________________ to medical school. I _______________________ work in a
(7)   (8)
hospital in the same neighborhood that I grew up in, and _______________________
(9)
I feel happy that I can give back to my community.

I am very grateful for the life I have now. Even though it is _______________________
(10)
that I arrived, sometimes that first day here seems like yesterday. _______________________
(11)
I still remember how terrified I felt _______________________ I took the
(12)
bus to school. _______________________ I wait for my young son's school bus
(13)
to arrive and watch him get on the bus. The freedom that I still cherish is normal for him.

_______________________ I intend to teach my son about the values of hard
(14)
work and the sacrifices that his grandparents made so that he can enjoy the world he lives in.

Vietnamese American Tet Festival in San Jose, California

Exercise 3.2 More Time Signals

A Complete sentences about yourself. Write about your life, for example, important events in your past and present and your hopes for the future.

1 I ____ for the first time in

____

2 By the time I was ____

I ____

3 Years later, I ____

4 After I ____

I ____

5 Over the past few years, I ____

6 I recently ____

7 Every day, I ____

8 In the next few years, I hope to ____

B Pair Work Share your sentences with a partner. Give more details.

I flew in a plane for the first time in 2002. I was 16 years old. I flew from Taiwan to Australia to see my aunt who had immigrated there. We spent a few days at a beach. It was so beautiful. We also went to a national park, and I saw koalas and kangaroos.

4 Avoid Common Mistakes ⚠

1   **Remember to use this/that with singular nouns and these/those with plural nouns.**
These
~~This~~ ideas about immigrants are common.

2   **Remember to use the in time signals such as *over the past year* and *in the next five years*.**
the
In ⌃ last five years, our neighborhood has become less diverse.

3   **Remember that frequency adverbs are usually placed before the main verb but after the verb *be*.**
never
He ~~never~~ has ⌃ seen so much traffic.
always
The traffic ~~always~~ is ⌃ bad.
He usually
~~Usually he~~ arrives late.

Editing Task

Find and correct eight more mistakes in the paragraph about an innovative device for the developing world.

The lack of clean drinking water is a problem in many parts of the world, but even when people have a source of water, collecting it can be arduous. Every morning, Isha gets water for her family. ~~Always it~~ *It always* takes her 30 minutes to get to the well and about an hour to walk back with a heavy clay container

5   of water balanced on top of her head. By time she returns, her body is aching from the weight of the water. She has been bringing water home like this for last 20 years. Isha lives in Niger, a country in West Africa. In Africa, women, and sometimes children, often are the ones responsible for collecting their family's water, and these responsibility takes a toll on their bodies. For some

10 women, the journey to a water source is very long. This women have to walk up to 18 miles (30 kilometers) a day for water. Hans Hendrikse, a native South African, wanted to do something about this problem. Working with his engineer brother, Pieter, he created a new way of transporting water. It is called the Q-Drum. The Q-Drum is lightweight, durable, and affordable, and it can hold 50 liters of water. While this features alone make the product

15 appealing, the most groundbreaking feature is its doughnut shape. When a rope is looped through the hole in the Q-Drum, the container can be rolled along the ground like a wheel. The Q-Drum's unique design allows even a young child to pull water for several miles, so the women never will have to carry the water solely on their heads. Over next decade this invention will have a major impact on the lives of the people of Africa, especially the women.

 Academic Writing

In this section, you will write a narrative essay. You will use a time line to organize your ideas. Before you start writing, you will learn about audience and purpose in narrative writing.

About Audience and Purpose

Whenever you write, you should always take into account who is going to be reading what you write. In other words, you should consider your audience. When you are writing an e-mail to friends to tell them about a recent trip, for example, you will probably use very informal language, such as contractions and slang. You probably won't worry about spelling and punctuation. However, the audience for a paper written for a college class would be very different. You would be much more careful about the kind of language that you use, the information that you provide, and your spelling and punctuation.

Here are some questions about audience for you to consider when you are planning your writing for a college class:

1 Who is my audience? Do I have multiple audiences (for example, a classroom teacher and an advisor)?

2 What do I want my audience to gain from reading the essay?

3 Am I writing for an audience who is likely to agree or disagree with my point of view? How does this affect the amount of detail I will provide and the type of language I use?

After deciding on the audience, a writer will need to determine the purpose of the writing. For an e-mail to friends about a recent trip, for example, the writer's purpose is likely to tell a story and entertain.

The purposes of writing for an audience could be:

- to entertain them;
- to teach them something new;
- to change their opinion;
- to change their behavior;
- to lead them to consider alternative options;
- to show your knowledge of a topic.

Exercise

A Match the texts on the next page to the appropriate audiences in the box. Write the number of the audience next to each text.

Audiences

1) a teacher   3) readers of an online magazine
2) classmates   4) a group of friends and relatives

Text 1

Are you considering moving to another country? If so, do your homework first. Here are two points you need to keep in mind:

1. Talk to as many people who live in the country as possible. They will be able to give you different perspectives of what life is like in the country.

2. Learn about actual costs. How much does it cost to rent an apartment or go food shopping? You need to know if you can afford living there.

Audience: _______

Text 2

Sorry I can't make this afternoon's meeting. Do you think it would be OK if we scheduled it for later in the week?

Thanks,

Audience: _______

Text 3

"Migration is a difficult concept to define because it includes people who move for different reasons across different spaces. A migrant can be a person who moves to another city or town within a nation; a refugee who crosses an international border to escape religious or political persecution; a jobseeker who moves to another country for better economic opportunities; a slave who is forcibly moved; or a person displaced by war or natural disaster. Demographers lack a single operational definition for migration because it occurs under different conditions" ("Migration – Types of Migration," n.d.).

Audience: _______

Text 4

I'm having lots of fun in Australia. I can't believe it's been six months already! I've made tons of friends. Sometimes I'm homesick, but oh, well . . . who isn't? I'll keep you updated about all the cool stuff I'm doing. Miss you all!

Audience: _______

B Pair Work Work with a partner and discuss the purpose of each of the texts in A. Share your ideas with another pair. Do you agree or disagree?

Pre-writing Tasks
Choose a Topic

A Choose one of the topics below. You will write an essay that contains a narrative that describes events that happened over several years.

- A success story

- A person who overcame difficulties

- A topic of your own approved by your teacher

B Pair Work Make a list of the main ideas and events to include in your essay. Share your ideas with a partner. Give each other suggestions about ideas to include.

Organize Your Ideas

A Creating a time line can help a writer organize the key events or information in the essay's narrative. On a separate sheet of paper, draw a time line similar to the one below and sequence the events that you will include in your essay.

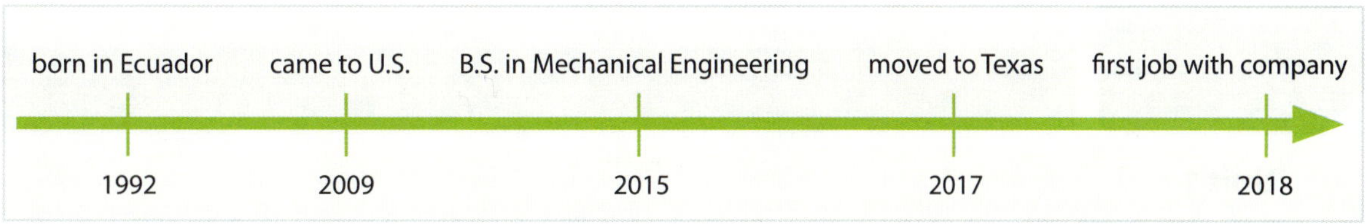

B Group Work Share your completed time line with a group. Encourage your group to ask you questions to help you explain and sequence the events in your story.

Writing Task

Write your essay. Follow the steps below.

1 Make sure you understand who your audience is.

2 Make sure that you understand the purpose of your paper before you start writing.

3 Include the following in your essay:

- *this / that / these / those* to connect ideas;
- common prepositional phrases and adverbs that signal time and sequence;
- at least three of these academic words from the essay in this unit: *approximately, challenge, contribute, distinct, economic, economy, immigrant, immigration, period, vary.*

4 After you write your essay, review it and make sure you avoided the mistakes in the Avoid Common Mistakes chart on page 154.

> **Academic Writing Tip**
>
> **Avoid Vague References**
>
> Make sure the noun referents of your demonstratives are clear.
>
> *Some scholars claim that economic disparity results in increased immigration.* **This** *is a significant problem for many countries.*
>
> "This" is vague. What does "this" refer to? Economic disparity? Immigration? The claim?

Peer Review

A Exchange your essay with a partner. Answer the following questions as you read your partner's essay, and then share your responses.

1 Who is the audience for the essay?

2 What is the purpose of the essay?

3 Did the writer use demonstratives?

4 Did the writer use time signals? Underline the ones the writer used.

5 Is anything confusing? Write a question mark (?) next to it.

6 Provide one compliment (something you found interesting or unusual).

B Use your partner's comments to help you revise your essay. Use the Writer's Checklist on page A2 to review your essay for organization, grammar, and vocabulary.

References

Unit 1

BBC. (2017). Albatrosses are ingesting plastic [Video file]. *Blue Planet II: Episode 7 Preview*. Retrieved from https://www.youtube.com/watch?v=I4QNoIP7Khc

BP. (2019). *BP Statistical Review of World Energy: 68th edition*. Retrieved from https://www.bp.com/content/dam/bp/business-sites/en/global/corporate/pdfs/energy-economics/statistical-review/bp-stats-review-2019-full-report.pdf

Morrison, D. & Tyree, C. (2017). Invisibles: the plastic inside us. Retrieved from https://orbmedia.org/stories/Invisibles_plastics/multimedia

Unit 2

Perner, L. (2008). Consumer behavior. *USC Marshall*. Retrieved from http://www.consumerpsychologist.com/intro_Consumer_Behavior.html

United States Environmental Protection Agency. (2019, August 15.) Paper and paperboard: material-specific data. Retrieved from https://www.epa.gov/facts-and-figures-about-materials-waste-and-recycling/paper-and-paperboard-material-specific-data

Unit 3

Murphy, C. (2019, July 12). Why social responsibility is important to businesses. *Investopedia*. Retrieved from https://www.investopedia.com/ask/answers/041015/why-social-responsibility-important-business.asp

Patagonia. (2019). Corporate responsibility. Retrieved from https://www.patagonia.com/corporate-responsibility.html

Waite, L. (2007). What makes a good corporate citizen? A discussion and case study. *EzineArticles.com*. Retrieved from http://ezinearticles.com/?What-Makes-a-Good-Corporate-Citizen?-A-Discussion-and-Case-Study&id=700539

Unit 4

Berke, J. (2018, May 8). One simple chart shows why an energy revolution is coming – and who is likely to come out on top. Retrieved from https://www.businessinsider.com/solar-power-cost-decrease-2018-5

BP energy outlook 2030. (2011). *BP*. Retrieved from http://www.bp.com/liveassets/bp_internet/globalbp/globalbp_uk_english/reports_and_publications/statistical_energy_review_2011/STAGING/local_assets/pdf/2030_energy_outlook_booklet.pdf

Energy today and tomorrow. (2008). *ACCENT*. Retrieved from http://www.atmosphere.mpg.de/enid/Nr2JuneO5_Context_4pu.html

Evans, S. (2007). The benefits of wind power. *Green Living Ideas*. Retrieved from https://greenlivingideas.com/2007/10/12/the-benefits-of-wind-power/

Our dependence on oil. (2010). *Environmental Defense Fund*. Retrieved from
http://apps.edf.org/page.cfm?tagID=58983

Ritchie, H. (2017, August 8). How long before we run out of fossil fuels? *Our World in Data*.
Retrieved from https://ourworldindata.org/how-long-before-we-run-out-of-fossil-fuels

Sweet, P. (2007). Insiders see solar energy industry as ready for takeoff. *Las Vegas Sun*.
Retrieved from http://www.lasvegassun.com/news/2007/aug/19/insiders-see-solar
-energy-industry-as-ready-for-ta/

The true costs of petroleum: The community map. (2003). *Ecology Center*. Retrieved from
http://ecologycenter.org/erc/petroleum/community.html

United Nations Environment Programme. (2019, June 18) Renewable energy investment
in 2018 hit USD 288.9 billion, far exceeding fossil fuel investment [Press release]. Retrieved
from https://www.unenvironment.org/news-and-stories/press-release/renewable-energy-
investment-2018-hit-usd-2889-billion-far-exceeding

Unit 5

Kochan, M. (2006). Birth order and adult sibling relationships. *Revolution Health Group*.
Retrieved from www.revolutionhealth.com/healthy-living/relationships/friends-family/
parents-siblings/birth-order

Petersen, A. (2010). A dose of sibling rivalry. *The Wall Street Journal*. Retrieved from
http://online.wsj.com/article/SB10001424052748704388504575419444247971432.html

Unit 6

Bureau of Labor Statistics. (2019, June 19). American time use survey summary [News release].
Retrieved from BLS website http://www.bls.gov/news.release/atus.nr0.htm

Catalyst. (2019, August 13). Pyramid: women in S&P companies. Retrieved from
https://www.catalyst.org/research/women-in-sp-500-companies/

IWPR. (2019, March). The gender wage gap: 2018 earnings differences by race and ethnicity.
Institute for Women's Policy Research. Retrieved from https://iwpr.org/wp-content/
uploads/2019/03/C478_Gender-Wage-Gap-in-2018.pdf

Unit 7

Clutter, A., & Nieto, R. (2009). Understanding the Latino culture. Retrieved from
http://citeseerx.ist.psu.edu/viewdoc/download?doi=10.1.1.183.6912&rep=rep1&type=pdf

Dr. Spock: Cultural differences in parenting. (n.d.). *Parents: Healthy Kids, Happy Families*.
Retrieved from http://www.parents.com/parenting/better-parenting/teaching
-tolerance/cultural-differences-parenting/

Unit 8

Galanti, G. (2000). An introduction to cultural differences. *The Western Journal of Medicine,
172*(5), 335–336.

Unit 9

Davis, S., Jenkins, G., & Hunt, R. (2003). *The pact: Three young men make a promise and fulfill a dream*. New York, NY: Riverhead Books.

Rodriguez, G. (2010). The American dream: Is it slipping away? *Los Angeles Times*. Retrieved from http://articles.latimes.com/2010/sep/27/opinion/la-oe-rodriguez-dream-20100927

Unit 10

Diner, H. (2008). Immigration and U.S. history. *America.gov*. Retrieved from https://www.ncpedia.org/anchor/immigration-us-history

Economic impact of immigration in the twentieth century. (2011). *DISCovering Collection*. Gale. Retrieved from Portland Community College website https://library.pcc.edu

European Migration Network. (2018). AMN annual report on migration and asylum 2017 – Sweden. Retrieved from https://ec.europa.eu/home-affairs/sites/homeaffairs/files/17a_sweden_arm_part2_2017_en.pdf

Migration – types of migration, theories on migration, migration and the family, migration and the global economy. (n.d.). *The Marriage and Family Encyclopedia*. JRank. Retrieved from http://family.jrank.org/pages/1173/Migration.html

Appendices

1 Parts of an Essay

<table>
<tr><td>INTRODUCTORY PARAGRAPH</td><td>Elements of Academic Writing

Writing in an academic style is necessary to succeed in school and in many jobs. **Nevertheless, this type of writing can seem overwhelming to students, who are used to a more informal style of writing, such as texting.** Understanding the key elements of academic writing can make it easier to manage. **Effective academic writing requires strong academic vocabulary, reliable sources, and clear organization.**</td><td>◄— **Hook** – draws reader in

Thesis Statement – gives main idea</td></tr>
<tr><td>BODY PARAGRAPH 1</td><td>**Using the right vocabulary is essential.** Writers should use precise and formal vocabulary to explain their ideas. For example, in conversation someone might say, "Sometimes kids have too much stuff to do, and they can't study." In academic writing, this might be expressed as, "Sometimes students have too many commitments, so it can be difficult for them to study." One resource that can help students build their academic vocabulary is the Academic Word List **(Coxhead, 2000)**, which identifies vocabulary that is commonly found in all disciplines. Some of these words include *achieve*, *potential*, and *similar*.</td><td>◄— **Topic Sentence**

Supporting Details

Citation – shows the source of the information</td></tr>
<tr><td>BODY PARAGRAPH 2</td><td>**Another important skill is researching and citing sources.** Academic writers should use reliable sources in their research and avoid sources that are biased. Writers must also avoid plagiarism by including the sources of all outside information. In academic writing, not providing a source of information is like cheating and can lead to serious consequences.</td><td>◄— **Topic Sentence**

Supporting Details</td></tr>
<tr><td>BODY PARAGRAPH 3</td><td>**It is also necessary to organize ideas appropriately.** Typically, essays contain an introductory paragraph, body paragraphs with supporting details, and a concluding paragraph that summarizes or restates the main points. In addition, different writing assignments, such as research reports and persuasive arguments, can have different patterns of organization. Good writers choose patterns that are appropriate for their purpose in writing.</td><td>◄— **Topic Sentence**

Supporting Details</td></tr>
<tr><td>CONCLUDING PARAGRAPH</td><td>In sum, academic essays have precise and formal vocabulary, information that is cited, and a clear organizational pattern. When writers understand the elements of academic writing, they become more effective writers. Mastering this skill can benefit students in college and, later, professionally.</td><td></td></tr>
<tr><td>REFERENCES</td><td>References
Coxhead, A. (2000). "A new academic word list." *TESOL Quarterly 34*(2): 213–238.</td><td></td></tr>
</table>

2 Writer's Checklist

		Yes	No
Audience	1. Is it clear who my audience is?		
	2. Is there anything I could do to make it clearer who my audience is?		
Purpose	1. Does my writing show that I understood the writing assignment?		
	2. Is the genre (cause and effect, problem–solution) clear?		
Length	Have I stayed within the minimum/maximum length?		
Organization	1. Did I follow my outline or other organizational structure I created for the writing assignment?		
	2. For paragraph writing assignments:		
	a. Does each paragraph have a topic sentence and address one main idea?		
	b. Do I support my topic sentence with clear examples, facts, and explanations?		
	3. For essay writing assignments:		
	a. Does the introductory paragraph introduce the topic?		
	b. Is there a hook that works well?		
	c. Do I have a clear thesis statement?		
	d. Does the essay address the topic and the thesis statement?		
	e. Do I have an effective conclusion?		
	4. Have I effectively used the writing point from this unit?		
Grammar	1. Do all my sentences have subjects and verbs?		
	2. Do all the subjects and verbs agree in number?		
	3. Are the forms of verbs correct?		
Vocabulary	1. Have I used the correct forms of words (e.g., the noun form or the adjective form)?		
	2. Have I avoided informal vocabulary or slang?		
	3. Are my vocabulary choices specific and clear?		
	4. Have I used connectors, such as demonstratives (*this, that,* etc.), transition words and phrases (*Therefore, However, In addition,* etc.), and pronouns (*it, they,* etc.), to connect ideas?		
Sources	1. Have I cited information that is from outside sources?		
	2. Is it clear to my reader what the source for each idea is?		
Your Questions	1.		
	2.		

3 About Plagiarism

Definition of Plagiarism

Plagiarism is considered a form of stealing in which a writer uses another writer's ideas and/or words improperly. As a writer, you plagiarize when you:

1. copy exact words from a source without noting the name of the source and using quotation marks.
2. paraphrase in a way that is too similar to the writer's original wording, i.e., when you replace only a few words in a sentence with synonyms.
3. state specific information, for example, unique ideas, results of a study or statistics, without identifying its source.

Reasons to Avoid Plagiarism

Plagiarism is a serious offense because it is considered to be both dishonest and unethical. Educational institutions have strict policies concerning plagiarism. Students who plagiarize could risk a failing grade or even being expelled. Therefore, it is essential for you to find out all you can about your school's policies on plagiarism and learn strategies to avoid plagiarizing.

There are other important reasons to avoid plagiarism. Writers typically feel a sense of ownership about their writing, especially when they have spent a lot of time and effort to do research and to create original and effective material. Citing a writer's ideas and original text is a way to respect the person's contributions. While many people talk about plagiarism as an issue of ownership, in the end, it may be more useful to think of it as "intellectual honesty."

Another reason involves your effectiveness as a writer. Taking language without paraphrasing it or ideas without citing them may create a false sense of your understanding of the information. In other words, when you cut and paste information from someone's work into your essay, you may not really understand the information, and you may use it improperly. Also, if questioned about the material, you may not be able to respond effectively.

Finally, when a writer uses language or ideas from another source without identifying that source, it makes it difficult for the reader to find out more information about what you have written and about the topic. The citations connect readers to credible sources of information.

How to Avoid Plagiarism

Whenever you use a writer's original words or ideas in your essay, you must credit the source in the text and in a reference list that follows your essay. In order to avoid plagiarism:

1. Use quotation marks around exact words from a source and cite the source in the text using APA or MLA style. This book uses APA style in citing in-text sources, e.g., (Brooks, 2010, p. 3).
2. Paraphrase (restate in your own words) the sentences that you want to include and cite the source in the text. See Unit 4 pp. 60–61 for a list of paraphrasing strategies.
3. Cite the source of a unique idea or specific information, such as a statistic.
4. Include a reference list at the end of your essay that has an entry for each citation in your essay.

How to Identify Plagiarism

Original Source	Excerpts From Students' Writing	Is This Plagiarism?
Primary and secondary characteristics of culture (Purnell & Paulanka, 2005, pp. 2–3) Major influences that shape people's worldview and the extent to which people identify with their cultural group of origin are called the primary and secondary characteristics of culture. The primary characteristics are nationality, race, color, gender, age, and religious affiliation. For example, two people have the same gender, age, nationality, and race, but if one is a devout Roman Catholic and the other is an Orthodox Jew, they may vary significantly in their health-care beliefs and practices. The secondary characteristics include educational status, socioeconomic status, occupation, military experience, political beliefs, urban versus rural residence, enclave identity, marital status, parental status, physical characteristics, sexual orientation, gender issues, reason for migration (sojourner, immigrant, or undocumented status), and amount of time away from the country of origin. Immigration status also influences a person's worldview. For example, people who voluntarily immigrate generally acculturate and more easily assimilate. Sojourners who immigrate with the intention of remaining in their new homeland for only a short time or refugees who think they may return to their home country may not have the need to acculturate or assimilate. Additionally, undocumented individuals (illegal immigrants) may have a different worldview from those who have arrived legally with work visas or as "legal immigrants."	Major influences that shape people's worldview and the extent to which people identify with their cultural group of origin are called the primary and secondary characteristics of culture.	**Yes**. This is copied directly from the source without quotation marks or a citation.
	"The primary characteristics [of culture] are nationality, race, color, gender, age, and religious affiliation" (Purnell & Paulanka, 2005, p. 2).	**No**. It includes quotation marks around exact text from the original source and a citation.
	For example, even with other characteristics being very similar, "a devout Roman Catholic and . . . an Orthodox Jew . . . may vary significantly in their health-care beliefs and practices."	**Yes**. Even though the statement is in quotation marks, the original source is not cited.
	Some secondary characteristics of culture include military service and political beliefs (Purnell & Paulanka, 2005).	**No**. It includes general ideas from the original source and a citation.
	Neither sojourners nor refugees may feel the need to acculturate or assimilate because they both believe that they may return to their home country (Purnell & Paulanka, 2005, p. 3).	**Yes**. Even though there is a citation, the words are still too close to the original. Acceptable: Sojourners and refugees may resist acculturation and assimilation because they see the move as only temporary. (Purnell & Paulanka, 2005, p. 3).

Final Points About Plagiarism

1. One good strategy to avoid plagiarizing is to take notes about your source rather than copying and pasting from the original to your own document. Then use your notes to write the important ideas from the source, as you understand them, without looking at the original source until you have finished.

2. Always remember to make a list of the sources. Follow the style (APA, MLA) that is preferred by your school, and make sure that you include information such as the author, year of publication, title, page or paragraph number in which you found the information, publisher and website for each source. Cut and paste urls from the websites into a document to help you keep track of them. This will also make it easier to create citations in your text and build your reference list.

3. Put quotation marks and mark the page number for *any* text that you have taken directly from a source, even if it is in your notes.

4. Just using good paraphrasing does not eliminate the risk of plagiarism because you need to include the source of ideas in the form of a citation, in addition to the paraphrase.

5. Plagiarism can be confusing for student writers because different readers, such as their instructors, may feel differently about how close is *too close,* in terms of either the source material's language or the original writer's ideas. It is always a good idea to check with your instructor for specific guidelines on plagiarism.

Glossary of Grammar and Writing Terms

active sentence a sentence that focuses on the doer and the action.
People spoke English at the meeting.

adjective a word that describes or modifies a noun.
Large ecological footprints cause problems.

adjective clause *see* **relative clause**

adverb a word that describes or modifies a verb, another adverb, or an adjective. Adverbs often end in -*ly*.
*Consumers need to shop **wisely**.*

adverb clause a clause that shows how ideas are connected. Adverb clauses begin with subordinators such as *because, since, although,* and *even though*.
*Some consumers purchase products they do not need **because they are on sale**.*

adverb clause of concession a clause that is used to contrast two things or ideas and particularly to indicate that the idea in the main clause is surprising. Adverb clauses of concession are introduced by the subordinators *although, even though, though,* and *while*.
***Even though face-to-face communication is preferred**, sometimes business has to be conducted virtually.*

adverb clause of contrast a clause that is used to contrast two things or ideas. Adverb clauses of contrast are introduced by the subordinators *while* and *whereas*.
*The official language of Brazil is Portuguese, **while in Colombia, it is Spanish**.*

adverb clause of purpose a clause that answers the question *why*. Adverb clauses of purpose are most often introduced by the subordinator *so that*, or just *so*.
*He cut down on fatty food **so (that) he could lose weight**.*

adverb of degree an adverb that makes other adverbs or adjectives stronger or weaker.
*Solar energy is **very** clean.*

adverb of manner an adverb that describes how an action happens.
*People can get into debt **easily**.*

adverb of time an adverb that describes when something happens.
*Firstborns are generally smarter than siblings who are born **later**.*

agent the noun or pronoun performing the action of the sentence.
*An **interviewer** screens candidates.*

appositive a noun phrase that either defines, restates, or gives important additional information about the noun phrase it follows.
*John Holland, **a leading researcher in vocational psychology**, developed a theory about career choices.*

article the words *a/an* and *the*. An article introduces or identifies a noun.
***A** new family moved in across **the** street from my house.*

auxiliary verb (also called **helping verb**) a verb that is used before a main verb in a sentence. *Do, have, be,* and *will* can act as auxiliary verbs.

*Natural resources **are** becoming scarce.*

*The Earth **does** not have time to renew the resources.*

base form of the verb the form of a verb without any endings (*-s* or *-ed*) or *to.*

come   go   take

citation a statement of the source of information cited, or used, in an essay. It includes who wrote the original material and/or what publication the original material came from.

" 'Car culture,' both in the cities and suburbs, causes the smog that helps make many California cities unhealthful" **("The True Costs of Petroleum: The Community Map," 2003)**.

citing (in essay writing) stating who wrote the original material and/or what publication the original material came from.

*Producing 20 percent of its energy from wind power, Denmark is the world leader in wind energy production **(Evans, 2007)**.*

clause a group of words that has a subject and a verb. There are two types of clauses: **independent clauses** and **dependent clauses**. A sentence can have more than one clause.

INDEPENDENT CLAUSE   DEPENDENT CLAUSE

***Future generations will suffer if pollution is not reduced**.*

cohesive device a device that a writer uses to connect back to previously stated ideas or information. Cohesive devices include pronouns, demonstratives, repetitions of words and phrases, different word forms, synonyms, and signal words and transition words.

*Visual learners are defined as people who learn through seeing. **For this reason, these** learners need to see the teacher's facial expressions to fully understand the content of a lesson.* (transition expression, demonstrative)

comma splice two independent clauses combined with a comma. To correct a comma splice, you can use a period between the two independent clauses.

Humans cause many environmental problems, it is our responsibility to resolve them. (comma splice)

Humans cause many environmental problems. It is our responsibility to resolve them. (correction)

comparative the form of an adjective or adverb that shows how two things or ideas are different.

*Immigrants in the United States often have **larger** families than Americans.* (adjective)

*Some people talk **more quickly** than others.* (adverb)

complex noun phrase a noun phrase that includes modifiers, such as adjectives, prepositional phrases, and relative clauses.

ADJECTIVE NOUN RELATIVE CLAUSE

*Sometimes **professional women who start their own businesses** have trouble getting loans.*

complex sentence a sentence with an independent clause and a dependent clause introduced by a subordinator.

INDEPENDENT CLAUSE   DEPENDENT CLAUSE

Bikeshares are becoming popular because they are a great way to reduce pollution.

compound sentence a sentence with at least two independent clauses that are connected by a coordinating conjunction (*and, but, or, so, yet*). Use a comma before the coordinating conjunction.

There are efforts to clean up the oceans, but the health of our oceans remains critical.

concluding paragraph the last paragraph in an essay in which the writer tries to make an impact. The writer may link back to ideas in previous paragraphs, ask a thought-provoking question, discuss potential consequences, or include a relevant quote.

conditional a sentence that describes a possible situation and the result of that situation. It can be a real or unreal condition/result about the present, past, or future. The possible situation, or the condition, is in the *if* clause.
> ***If companies recycle, employees generally recycle, too***. (present real conditional)
> ***If I had read the privacy policy carefully, I would have avoided the problem.*** (past unreal conditional)

coordinating conjunction a word such as *and, but, so, or,* and *yet* that connects single words, phrases, or clauses.
> *Some gases trap heat in the air,* **so** *the Earth gets warmer.*

count noun refers to a person, place, or thing you can count. Count nouns have a plural form and take plural verbs.
> *Large* **families** *are enjoyable.*

definite article the word *the*. Use *the* with a noun when both the reader and the writer share common knowledge or information about the noun, when the noun is unique, or when the noun was introduced earlier.
> *In American families, it is common for* **the** *wife and* **the** *husband to share household duties.*
> **The** *president spoke about mobility in U.S. society.*
> *Each person in a family has a moral responsibility to aid other members of* **the** *family.*

demonstrative the words *this, that, these, those*. Demonstratives are used to show physical distance from the speaker, to show distance in time, or to connect ideas that are close to each other in a text.
> *Chapter 2 is about immigration. In* **this** *chapter, the author describes immigration in the mid-1800s.*
> *Immigrants came from all over Europe. Most of* **these** *immigrants became farmers.*

dependent clause a clause that cannot stand alone. A dependent clause is not a complete sentence, but it still has a subject and verb. Some kinds of dependent clauses are adverb clauses, relative clauses, and time clauses.
> ***Although people try to save energy,*** *global use of it increases every year.*

determiner a word that comes before a noun to limit its meaning in some way. Some common determiners are *some, a little, a lot, a few, this, that, these, those, his, a/an, the, much,* and *many*.
> **This** *unit is about immigration. Let's look at* **the** *first page.*
> **A** *young Latina woman is* **the** *new student in* **my** *class.*
> **Few** *women are CEOs.*

direct object the person or thing that receives the action of the verb.
> *An interviewer screened the* **candidates***.*

direct speech (also called **quoted speech**) repetition of a person's exact words. A direct speech statement consists of a reporting clause and the exact words of a person inside quotation marks.
> ***The manager said, "Workers need to use creativity."***

-ed phrase a phrase that begins with a past participle that acts as an adjective and modifies a noun.
> *Women* **elected to Congress** *are in the minority.*

element a part of a sentence that works as a grammatical unit, such as a subject, a verb, an object, an adjective, an adverb, or a prepositional phrase.

SUBJECT   VERB PREPOSITIONAL PHRASE

The topic of greenhouse gases is often in the news.

formal a style of writing or speech used when it is not appropriate to show familiarity, such as in business interactions, a job interview, speaking to a stranger, or speaking to a person who you respect. Academic writing is a kind of formal writing.

Good evening. I'd like to speak with Ms. Smith. Is she available?

Swanson (2010) has argued that labeling may be a short-term solution to the problem of GM foods.

fragment an incomplete sentence in which the subject or verb is missing. Avoid fragments by making sure all sentences have a subject and a verb.

In the future, will probably be much warmer on Earth. (fragment, missing subject)

frequency adverb an adverb that describes how often an action happens.

*Ozone and other greenhouse gases are **often** debated in the news.*

future a number of verb forms that describe a time that has not yet happened. The future is expressed in English by *will, be going to*, modals, and a variety of words and phrases.

*The Internet **will continue to** allow for a greater exchange of ideas.*

*Some colleges **are going to** ban access to social networking sites on campus.*

*The use of social networking sites by recruiters for jobs **could increase** in the next few years.*

*The company **is about to** introduce a new app.*

future real conditional a sentence that describes a possible situation or condition in the future and its likely result. The verb in the *if* clause is in the simple present, and the verb in the main clause is *be going to* or a modal such as *will* or *might*.

If I get a raise, we will be able to buy a new car.

future unreal conditional a sentence that describes an imaginary situation in the future and gives the result as if it were true. The verb in the *if* clause is in the past, and the verb in the main clause includes one of these modals: *would, could, might*.

If we were socially responsible, we would attract more customers.

gerund the *-ing* form of a verb that is used as a noun. It can act as a subject or object.

***Reducing** our ecological footprints is crucial.*

habitual past a verb form that describes repeated past actions, habits, and conditions using *used to* or *would*.

*I **used to** study on the bus to school every day.*

*While I was living in my country, I **would** go for long walks.*

helping verb see **auxiliary verb**.

hook a part of an essay that tries to interest readers and motivate them to keep reading the essay. Hooks may be a surprising fact, a thought-provoking question, or a quotation. The hook is usually the first or second sentence in the introductory paragraph.

identifying relative clause a relative clause that modifies a noun and gives necessary information about the noun. Without that information, the sentence would be incomplete. Do not use commas with identifying relative clauses.

*The study examines characteristics **that are common in firstborn children**.*

_if_ clause the condition clause in a conditional. It describes the possible situation, which can be either real or unreal.

**If a company does not make a profit**, it will go bankrupt.

imperative a type of clause that tells people to do something. It may give instructions, directions to a place, or advice. The verb is in the base form.

**Listen** to the conversation.

**Don't open** your books.

indefinite article _a/an_ is the indefinite article. Use _a/an_ with a singular count noun when the noun is not specifically identified or when it is first mentioned and new to the reader. Use _a_ with consonant sounds. Use _an_ with vowel sounds.

There is **a** new student in my class.

The class read **an** article about cultural values.

indefinite pronoun a pronoun used when the noun is unknown or not important. There is an indefinite pronoun for people, for places, and for things. Some examples are _somebody, anyone, nobody, one, somewhere, anywhere, nothing, everything,_ etc. Use singular verb forms when the indefinite pronoun is the subject of the sentence.

**Nobody** in her family had ever attended college before.

First, **one** needs to acknowledge that a problem exists.

independent clause (also called **main clause**) a clause that can be used alone as a complete sentence.

Although people try to save energy, **global demand for energy increases every year**.

indirect object the person or thing that receives the direct object.

Many merchants offer **consumers** green products.

indirect speech (also called **reported speech**) tells what someone says in another person's words. An indirect speech statement consists of a reporting verb (_see_ **reporting verb**) such as _say_ in the main clause, followed by a _that_ clause. The word _that_ is optional and is often omitted in speaking.

**The expert said (that) junk food was unhealthy.**

informal a style of speaking and writing used to communicate with friends, family, or children.

Hey, there. Nice to see you again.

infinitive _to_ + the base form of a verb.

It is difficult **to find** time to exercise every day.

infinitive of purpose an infinitive that answers the question _why_. Infinitives of purpose can be introduced by _in order to_ and _so as to_. If the meaning is clear, it is not necessary to use _in order_.

Doctors place brochures in their waiting rooms **(in order) to provide** patients with valuable information.

Doctors should discuss treatment options with patients **so as to address** any concerns.

-ing participle phrase a phrase that begins with the _-ing_ form of a verb. It can act as an adjective and modify a noun or it can express cause and effect.

The number of women **starting their own businesses** is increasing. (adjective modifying a noun)

**Using wind energy**, we can lower the cost of electricity. (cause)

Some countries give tax credits for wind energy, **lowering costs for consumers**. (effect)

***it* construction** a construction such as *it + be +* adjective *+ that* clause, *it + be +* adjective *+ infinitive*, *it + appears/seems + that* clause, *it + appears/seems +* adjective *+ that* clause. These constructions are commonly used in academic writing to make the text more impersonal and objective.

***It is true that** people who exercise usually have more energy.*

***It is important to find** an exercise that is enjoyable.*

***It seems that** people who eat healthier are frequently in a good mood.*

main clause *see* **independent clause**.

main verb a verb that functions alone in a clause and can have an auxiliary verb.

*Solar energy **is** very clean.*

*The government is **investing** large sums of money in alternative energy projects.*

modal a verb such as *can, may, should,* and *will*. It goes before the main verb to show such things as ability, permission, possibility, advice, obligation, necessity, or lack of necessity.

*We **might** buy a hybrid car.*

*The gifts **should** not be expensive.*

modal-like expression a verb such as *have to, be going to,* and *be supposed to* that acts like a modal but changes its form of the verb.

*The country **had to** change its policies.*

*She **was supposed to** major in education, but she decided to change her major to economics.*

modifier a word or a phrase that is added to another phrase to change or describe it. Adjectives, prepositional phrases, and adverbs are examples of modifiers.

*Receptions **for weddings** involve **delicious** foods.* (prepositional phrase, adjective)

*They **commonly** involve music.* (adverb)

noncount noun ideas and things that you cannot count. Noncount nouns do not have a plural form and so use a singular verb.

*My cousin borrowed some **money** from me.*

nonidentifying relative clause a relative clause that provides additional information about a noun. The sentence would be complete without the information in the relative clause. Use commas with a nonidentifying relative clause.

*National Institute of Mental Health, **which is a government agency,** conducts research on the effects of violence on children.*

noun a word for a person, place, or thing.

*Some **consumers** buy "green" **products**.*

noun clause a clause that acts as a noun and that can be the subject or object in a sentence. Noun clauses often start with *that*. They can also start with *wh-* words and *if/whether*.

*Experts suggest **that the consumption of fast food has increased**.*

*Readers have to decide **which experts they trust**.*

*Students who use online sources should check **whether the sources are reliable or inaccurate**.*

noun clause with *wh-* words a clause that starts with a *wh-* word (*who, what, where, when, why,* and *how*). These noun clauses function as nouns and can act as subjects, objects, or objects of prepositions. They use statement word order.

*Students have to learn **how they can evaluate sources**.*

*Experts disagree on **what the benefits of Internet use are for students**.*

noun phrase a phrase that includes a noun and modifiers.

DETERMINER ADJECTIVE NOUN   PREPOSITIONAL PHRASE

*__The__ extremely **sensitive issue of gender inequality** has been discussed for many decades.*

object a noun or pronoun that receives the action and usually follows the verb.

*Many researchers study **families**. They analyze **them**.*

object relative clause a relative clause in which the relative pronoun is the object of the verb in the relative clause.

*There are several strategies **that parents can use to help their only children**.*

parallel structure a list in which each item follows the same grammatical pattern.

ADJECTIVE   ADJECTIVE   ADJECTIVE

*Boys are encouraged to be **aggressive, outgoing,** and **strong**.*

paraphrase to state the information in a different way from the original without changing its meaning.

"Denmark leads the world in wind energy, generating 20 percent of its energy from wind power" (Evans, 2007, para. 3).

*Paraphrase: **Denmark is the world leader in wind energy. Twenty percent of its energy comes from wind power. (Evans, 2007)***

passive a sentence that focuses on the action or on the person or thing that receives the action. The object is in the subject position. The verb form in the passive is a form of *be* + past participle.

The results of the survey were presented by the committee at the meeting.

past modal modals such as *had to/did not have to, should have/should not have, could have/could not have,* and *might have*. Speakers use these modals to give their perspective on past events.

*They **had to** find a way to pay for their education. (past necessity)*

*He **could have** found out about the job opening at the career center. (possible action in the past)*

past participle a verb form that can be regular (base form + *-ed*) or irregular. It is used to form perfect forms of the verb and the passive. It can also be an adjective.

*Researchers have **examined** the situation carefully.*

*Auditions are **known** to be effective interview tools.*

*The **increased** cost of housing has affected many students.*

past perfect a verb form that describes the first of two completed events in the past. It can also describe an action or situation that goes back to an earlier time in a narrative or description. In narrative and academic writing, it is used to give background reasons and explanations for later past events. Its form is *had* + past participle.

*By midnight, he **had finished** most of his work, so he decided to go to bed.*

*Nesreen was nervous on her first day of work. She**'d** never **had** a job before.*

*For years, many people **had considered** the American dream to be achievable. Then the economy changed.*

past perfect progressive a verb form that emphasizes an ongoing past action leading up to a point in the past or a past action that had been occurring when another action took place. Its form is *had* + *been* + verb + *-ing*.

*He**'d been talking** about applying to medical school for a long time. Finally, last January, he applied.*

*They**'d been working** for about an hour when the bell rang.*

past unreal conditional a sentence that describes a hypothetical situation – an untrue situation in the past. Past unreal conditionals describe something that was possible but did not happen. The verb in the *if* clause is in the past perfect. The verb in the main clause uses the modal *would have, could have,* or *might have* and the past participle form of the verb.

If the author had discussed education in his article, the text would have been stronger.

phrase a group of words about an idea that is not a complete sentence. It does not have a main verb.

about the environment

in the future

preposition a word such as *to, at, for, with, of, in, on,* or *above* that goes before a noun or pronoun to show location, time, or direction.

*Stores put snack foods **on** low shelves so that children can see and ask **for** them.*

prepositional phrase a phrase with a preposition and an object, which is usually a noun or pronoun. It can be part of a noun phrase or a verb phrase. Some reduced relative clauses are also prepositional phrases.

*The debate **on immigration** has heated up recently.*

*Immigration has increased **over the past 20 years**.*

present perfect a verb form that describes a past event that is still important in the present. This event may be completed, or it may continue into the future. The form is *have/has* + past participle.

*Some researchers **have demonstrated** that genetically modified food may cause damage to humans.*

*The consumption of GM foods **has increased** significantly in the last 10 years.*

present perfect progressive a verb form that describes an action that started in the past and emphasizes that the action continues to the present and may continue into the future. The form is *have/has* + *been* + verb + *-ing*.

*Researchers **have been studying** the impact of GM foods on our health.*

present real conditional a sentence that describes a possible situation or condition in the present and its likely result now. The verbs in the *if* clause and the main clause are in the simple present.

If companies donate to charity programs, they set good examples for other companies.

present unreal conditional a sentence that describes an imaginary situation in the present and gives the result. The verb in the *if* clause is in the past, and the verb in the main clause includes one of these modals: *would, could, might.*

If employees became involved in the community, they would feel good about themselves.

quantifier a word that indicates the amount or degree of something. Some examples of quantifiers are *all, almost all, most, several, some, few, both,* and *no.*

Most *toys are gender-specific.*

relative clause (also called **adjective clause**) modifies or describes a noun and follows the noun that it modifies. It begins with a relative pronoun such as *who, whom, which, that,* or *whose.*

*Children **who have siblings** are often very close to their parents.*

reporting verb a verb that writers use to report ideas or findings from a source. Reporting verbs are followed by *that* clauses or noun phrases. Common reporting verbs include *say, show, explain, mention, report,* and *state.*

*The authors of the study **conclude** that childhood obesity can be very harmful.*

run-on sentence two independent clauses that are not separated by a period, semicolon, or coordinating conjunction. To correct a run-on sentence, use a comma and a coordinating conjunction to connect the two independent clauses.

Gases trap heat in the air the Earth gets warmer. (run-on sentence)

Gases trap heat in the air, so the Earth gets warmer. (correction)

sentence a complete thought or idea that has a subject and a main verb. In writing, it begins with a capital letter and has a punctuation mark (. ? !) at the end.

The Earth is becoming warmer.

signal words words that help the reader know that the writer has finished writing about one step in the process and started writing about another. Signal words include words and phrases such as *first, the first thing to do, second, next, after that,* and *finally.*

simple sentence a sentence with only one clause, which is called an independent clause or a main clause. Like all sentences, it has a subject and a verb.

Small changes can make a difference.

subject the person, place, or thing that performs the action of a verb.

People *should buy less.*

subject relative clause a clause in which the relative pronoun is the subject of the verb in the relative clause.

*Researchers **who study families** have different views.*

subordinator (also called **subordinating conjunction**) a word that shows the relationship between the two ideas. It introduces an adverb clause. Some common subordinators are *before, after, while, because, since, if, although, whether, whereas,* and *as if.*

*Some consumers buy products **because** they want to be like their friends.*

superlative the form of an adjective or adverb that compares one thing or idea to others in a group.

*Latinos are currently one of **the largest** ethnic groups in the United States.* (adjective)

*Americans are among the groups who say things **the most directly**.* (adverb)

supporting detail a detail or example that explains or supports the main idea of the paragraph.

***that* clause** a clause that acts as a noun and that can be the subject or object in a sentence.

*The expert recommended **that people read food labels carefully**.*

thesis statement a sentence that states the main idea of an essay and gives a preview of what the writer is going to say about the topic. It is often the last sentence in the introductory paragraph.

time clause a clause that shows the order of events and begins with a subordinator such as *after, as, before,* and *while.*

After I finished high school, *I had to find a job.*

time signal a word or phrase that makes the sequence of events or ideas easier to follow. They are important in narrative writing. Common time signals are *after, over (the course of), by, for; already, always, ever, just, lately, never; every day, once, once again, twice; later, earlier.*

Over the next 10 years, *immigration is likely to decrease.*

*We've **always** lived in this neighborhood.*

Years later, *I returned to Boston to go to medical school.*

topic sentence a sentence that introduces the main idea of a body paragraph in an essay. It often appears at the beginning of a body paragraph.

transition word or phrase a word or phrase that connects two independent clauses to make the relationship between two ideas very clear. Transition words and phrases signal a number of different relationships, such as cause and effect, concession, contrast, and steps of a solution. Use a comma after a transition word or phrase.

Environmental values might affect some purchases; **consequently,** *merchants offer green products.*

U.S. executives prefer time limits for meetings. **In contrast,** *Greeks see them as less necessary.*

First, *it is important for people to find an activity that is enjoyable.* **Next,** *they need to commit to doing it.*

verb a word that describes an action or a state.

People **use** *a lot of resources in developed countries. Many of them* **know** *that they should reduce their ecological footprints.*

verb phrase a phrase that includes a main verb, any modals or auxiliary verbs, and elements such as adverbs, direct objects, and prepositional phrases.

VERB   PREPOSITIONAL PHRASE

Solar energy **will grow in importance***.*

Art Credits

Acknowledgements

The authors and publishers acknowledge the following sources of copyright material and are grateful for the permissions granted. While every effort has been made, it has not always been possible to identify the sources of all the material used, or to trace all copyright holders. If any omissions are brought to our notice, we will be happy to include the appropriate acknowledgements on reprinting and in the next update to the digital edition, as applicable.

Key: U = Unit

Photography

All the photos are sourced from Getty Images.

U1: LeoFFreitas/Moment; Gabriel Grams; JayLazarin/iStock/Getty Images Plus; **U2**: Jim Craigmyle/Corbis; Darryl Estrine/UpperCut Images; **U3**: RapidEye/E+; Martin Barraud/Caiaimage; Zinkevych/iStock/Getty Images Plus; **U4**: Aaaaimages/Moment; AFP Contributor; MyrKu/iStock/Getty Images Plus; Jens Schlueter/DDP; **U5**: WPA Pool; Brooks Kraft/Corbis Historical; Carsten Koall; Jessica Peterson; Scott Barbour; H. Armstrong Roberts/ClassicStock/Archive Photos; **U6**: nito100/iStock/Getty Images Plus; Hero Images; **U7**: Maskot; Hero Images; Hirurg/E+; Pixelchrome Inc/DigitalVision; **U8**: FatCamera/E+; Juice Images; **U9**: Anthony Barboza/Archive Photos; Hemant Mehta; Rubberball Productions; Astrid Stawiarz; Martin Mills/Hulton Archive; Oliver Gerhard; **U10**: Drew Angerer; Francis Dean/Corbis Historical; Tom Stoddart Archive/Hulton Archive.

The following photos are sourced from other libraries/sources.

U5: Hine, Lewis Wickes, 1874-1940/Library of Congress; **U10**: Calamy stock images/Alamy Stock Photo.

Illustrations

Bill Dickson; Monika Roe; Rob Schuster; Shelton Leong.

Audio

Audio production by John Marshall Media

Typeset by Q2A Media Services Pvt. Ltd.